THE WESTERN RISING
1549

THE PRAYER BOOK REBELLION

PHILIP CARAMAN

**WESTCOUNTRY
BOOKS**

First published in 1994 by Westcountry Books
Copyright © 1994 Philip Caraman

ISBN 1 898386 03 X

British Library Cataloguing- in -Publication Data
CIP data for this book is available from the British Library

WESTCOUNTRY BOOKS
Lower Moor Way
Tiverton
Devon EX16 6SS
0884 243242
0884 243325

Printed and bound in Great Britain by Bookcraft Ltd,
Midsomer Norton.

CONTENTS

INTRODUCTION

The History of Exeter by John Hooker or Vowell, the father of Richard Hooker the apologist of the Elizabethan Religious Settlement, remains today the principal source of our knowledge of the Western Rebellion of 1549. Born in 1526 Hooker was a young man of twenty-three at the time of the Rising. His purpose in writing was to set down 'the beginnings, cause and course of the commotion in the counties of Devon and Cornwall'. A native of Exeter and the son of a Mayor of the city he had been familiar from his youth with some of the most influential citizens. As a pupil of Dr John Moreman, the enlightened vicar of Menheniot in Devon, he went to Oxford where he became a Fellow of Corpus Christi. In his travels on the Continent he lived for a time at Strasbourg with Pietro Martire, known in England as Peter Martyr, the Italian reformer, who at the time of the Rising was Regius Professor of Divinity at Oxford.

Though Hooker's Protestant standpoint is never in doubt, his prejudices, when they appear, hardly affect the value of his narrative. As the historian of the Rising he had the inestimable advantage of being present in Exeter during the five weeks of its siege by the rebels: he rightly claims therefore to have been *testis oculatus* or eye witness 'of things then done'. He was able, moreover, to gather at first hand information from the government side, for he later became secretary and solicitor to Sir Peter Carew, the royalist commander who played a crucial role in the suppression of the rebellion.

Hooker wrote his account of the Rising because he regarded it as the most important event of the reign that 'had not been fully and at large set forth by any man', meaning, of course, writers like Strype on whom people depended for their knowledge of history. For this reason when he came to edit Holinshed's *Chronicle of England* in 1586, he published his history of the rebellion as an appendix to the Chronicle. In spite of widespread agrarian disturbances at the time in most parts of the country, Hooker is emphatic that the cause of the western rebellion 'was only concerning religion'; this was also the judgement of another contemporary, the chronicler Charles Wriothesley, who wrote in his account of the events of the year that 'the Devonshire men and the Cornishmen made insurrections against the King's proceedings to maintain the Mass and the ceremonies of the Pope's law'.

The Protestant Council under the Presidency of the Duke of Somerset that governed in the name of Edward VI treated the rebellion as a mortal threat to the progress of the Reformation and to the social order that supported it. Had the rebellion succeeded, as it so nearly did, it would have shaken the basis of the Protestant movement which became firmly established in the important remaining years of Edward VI's reign. The story of the Rising, together with evidence from elsewhere, goes to show that the religious changes under Edward VI were as little loved as the government that brought them in. And it could be argued that but for a fatal strategic error by the rebel leaders, their ill luck and their lack of cavalry, the history of religion in England could have been different.

I would perhaps be claiming too much to say that my motive in writing this book was the same as John Hooker's, namely, that today, as in his time, this chapter of English history, though it remains embedded in folk memory in the South West, has been allowed to fade into comparative obscurity. There is no need to go further for proof of this than the volume on the Early Tudors in the *Oxford History of England* where Professor Mackie dismisses the subject in six lines.

The last full treatment of the rebellion was the work of an American scholar, Frances Rose-Troup, published in 1913 and entitled *The Western Rebellion of 1549 : an account of the Insurrections in Devonshire and Cornwall against religious innovations in the reign of Edward VI.* This very thorough investigation of the subject, with its appended source material, is still a valuable work. More recently A.L. Rowse in his *Tudor Cornwall* (1941) has an excellent chapter on the subject in which he draws on his unrivalled knowledge of his native Cornwall. I am much indebted to these two authors and also to Julian Cornwall's *Revolt of the Peasantry* (1977) which concentrates on the military aspect of the Western and Norfolk Risings of 1549.

My main interest has been in the religious aspect of the Rebellion and I have accordingly tried to enter the mind of the people who took part in the rising and understand the strength of their attachment to their religious practice and faith which alone can account for the desperation with which they fought to the end against overwhelming odds.

Philip Caraman
Dulverton
January 1994

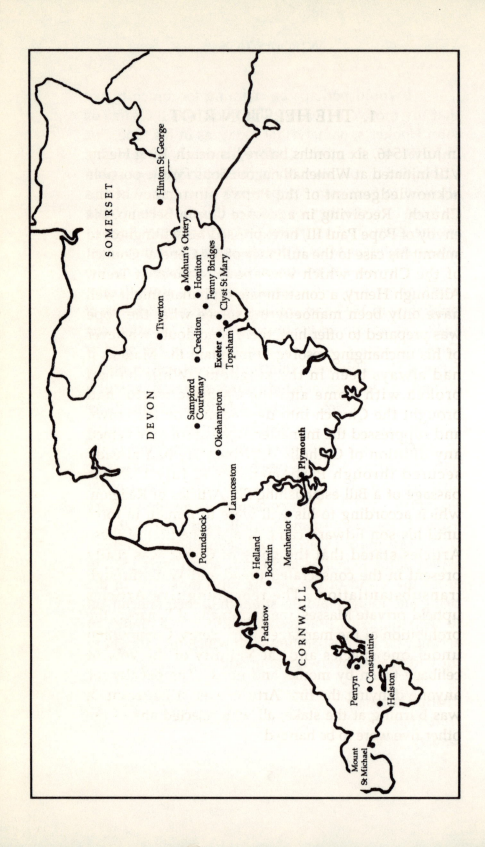

1. THE HELSTON RIOT

In July 1546, six months before his death, King Henry VIII initiated at Whitehall negotiations for the possible acknowledgement of the Pope's supremacy of the Church. Receiving in audience Guron Bertano, the envoy of Pope Paul III, he expressed his willingness to submit his case to the authority of the General Council of the Church which was about to meet at Trent. Although Henry, a consummate diplomat, might well have only been manoeuvring to see what the Pope was prepared to offer him, there is no doubt whatever of his unchanging resolve to maintain the Mass as it had always been in the kingdom. While he had broken with Rome and the Catholic world, had brought the Church into dependence on the crown and suppressed the monasteries, he absolutely vetoed any dilution of Catholic doctrine. He had already secured through Parliament on 12 July 1539 the passage of a Bill establishing Six Articles of Religion, which according to his will were to remain in force until his son Edward came of age. The first of these Articles stated that the body of Christ was really present in the consecrated Bread and Wine through transubstantiation. The remaining five Articles upheld private Masses, the sacrament of Penance, the prohibition of the marriage of the clergy, Communion under one species and the validity of the vow of celibacy taken by monks and nuns. The penalty for anyone denying the first Article, even if he recanted, was burning at the stake; all who rejected any of the other five were to be hanged.

5

Henry himself intervened in the debate in the House of Lords, arguing vehemently and successfully for the Six Articles against Cranmer who was consequently compelled to despatch his wife back to Germany. On the Continent the passage of the Bill was regarded as a victory over the Reformers. Two years later the King told Charles de Marillac, the French Ambassador, that he was even more strongly opposed to the marriage of the clergy than to papal supremacy on the grounds that if priests were permitted to marry benefices would become hereditary and the clergy form a powerful body that would threaten royal power.

When on the afternoon of 27 January 1547 the King lay dying at Whitehall he summoned Cranmer, who was then at Guildford, to hear his confession. There was a heavy frost that night across all northern Europe; the ice on the roads made progress slow and the Archbishop reached London in time only to elicit from the speechless King a sign that he trusted in the mercy of God. He died at two o'clock on the following morning.

Under the old King changes in religion had been introduced gradually. True, the payments previously made to Rome were now transferred to the Treasury and were more strictly enforced. But in the church services alterations had been neither radical nor extensive and in remoter parts of the kingdom like Lancashire and Cornwall they had been largely ignored. In the unessential parts of the Mass English had replaced Latin, but again this did not hold everywhere. The ritual still retained its ancient grandeur in the cathedrals and parish churches and the dull daily routine of the commons was still

6

relieved by the splendour of the ancient ritual. This was particularly true of Cornwall, the seat of the Western Rising and perhaps the poorest part of England: the food of the peasants was poor, their clothing rough and their houses built with earthen walls and thatched roofs and bedding consisted of heaped straw and a blanket.

In his homily at the coronation of the new King on 20 February Cranmer left the country in no doubt about his intention, as he told the nine year old Edward, 'to see idolatry destroyed, the tyranny of the bishops of Rome banished from your subjects and images destroyed', a programme which he set out in detail in his *Homily of Good Works* which was published in the following July: among the 'papistical superstitions and abuses' to be abolished were beads, the office of Our Lady, the rosary, Masses for the dead, jubilees, bells, holy water, palms, candles, fastings, fraternities and such like practices 'prejudicial to God's glory and commandments'.

In the following summer the Council ordered a visitation of the whole kingdom to enforce a series of Injunctions concerning religion: purporting to be no more than a restatement of decrees of Henry VIII, they went in fact much further: they ordered the destruction of all images, including those in windows, cancelled all fast and feast days, condemned any form of the recitation of the Rosary and forbade the burning of all lights apart from two on the altar: this last injunction led to the destruction of the figures of Christ, Mary and St John on the rood screen, and was the end of pious societies charged with the burning of lights before them; it was now only a step to the destruction of the screen itself and a radical change in the appearance of the churches: the priests moreover were ordered to exhort their people to do away with all images in their own homes.

More radical still, the Injunctions abolished all processions, not only the parish processions that preceded the principal Mass on Sundays, but all others, both inside and outside the church, including the processions on the feast of Corpus Christi and the three Rogation days.

The visitation which was to enforce the Injunctions began in September 1547 and was to continue into the next year. Before the middle of September, however, there was such a rash of window breaking in London churches that the Council, fearing riots, stepped in, ordering windows containing images of the Pope or Thomas Becket merely to be defaced or covered over and not to be smashed. In November the rood screen in St Paul's was removed during the night in order to avoid an outcry.

In the same month the first Parliament of Edward VI met under the presidency of the Duke of Somerset, the new King's maternal uncle and President of the Regency Council. A convinced Protestant, Somerset, as soon as the King had died, was in correspondence with Calvin who encouraged him to undertake a reformation of religion in England on the German pattern, ridding the churches of anything that in his judgement smacked of superstition. The new Protestant religion would have to be presented so as not to alienate the majority of the nation; it was to be determined by Parliament and there could be no question of tolerating any other form of worship. The first Protestant ruler of England, Somerset had amassed a huge fortune in monastic lands and on assuming power set about building Somerset House with materials from the old Clerkenwell Priory and the demolished cloister of St Paul's cathedral.

The first act of the new Parliament was to repeal Henry VIII's Six Articles of Religion and the Act *De Heretico Comburendo* of 1401 which compelled the burning of heretics at the stake, a measure which cleared the way for drastic innovations. There was a strong opposition in both Houses that resented what they regarded as an usurpation of royal authority, arguing that the headship of the Church was personal to the King and could not be transferred to a mixed body of men such as Parliament or the Council: it was also pointed out that the whole question of religious change should be in abeyance until the young King attained his majority. Nevertheless, the measure was passed and the way cleared for reform.

In December a new Chantries Act followed the repeal of the Six Articles. Already, two years previously, Parliament had allowed Henry VIII to appropriate some of these foundations, but only for his lifetime and with the exclusive purpose of defraying the cost of the war against France. After ordering a survey of the chantries Henry did in fact appropriate a number of them. But this new Act went much further. And worse, it was an undisguised Protestant measure with the avowed purpose, as its preamble stated, of doing away with 'superstitious practices and errors touching man's salvation' which had led to 'devising and fantasying vain opinions of Purgatory and Masses satisfactory to be done for them which be departed'. The King was to 'have and enjoy the goods, chattels, jewels, plate, ornaments and other moveables' belonging to all chantry chapels, and colleges and all the stipends of the priests serving them. Apart from irretrievably damaging the educational system of the country it affected the people more directly than had the suppression of the monasteries: the monasteries had been mainly in the country, but the chantries, often a chapel in a parish church or a cathedral, were in or near the towns and were receiving fresh endowments from the merchants and gentry well into the sixteenth century: in Exeter cathedral, for instance, the chapel of St George was built as the chantry of the Speke family in the year 1517 and contained the tomb and effigy of Sir John Speke of Whitelackington. Frequently the endowments were in the form of real estate and made for the support of a priest to offer Mass for the founder and his kin in perpetuity, usually at a particular altar or chapel and often with the attached duty of teaching the young or ministering to the sick or aged. With the exception of the privileged City of London companies, the Act suppressed all free chapels, colleges, hospitals, fraternities and similar institutions.

At a single stroke the Act snatched from the people their treasured link with the departed members of their family. It has been pointed out that 'if a man really believed that the ministration of a chantry priest shortened the bitter years of Purgatory for himself and his dearest departed relatives, then the Dissolution gave him great spiritual offence and became a matter for his passionate concern'.[1]

Moreover, as a recent historian has observed, the Act deprived the parishes throughout the country of their auxiliary clergy who assisted in the liturgy, took charge of the singing on Sundays and feasts and helped to shrive and give communion to the people at Easter. At Ashburton in Devon, for instance, where the burgesses formed the thriving guild of St Lawrence, the people lost, all at the same time, control over their market, the endowments of their parochial school, the funds used for supplying water to the town, for the care of their sick and the support of the clergy serving the parish church. (2)

Moreover, 'the King this year (1548)', writes Hooker, 'sent out commissioners throughout the realm for the defacing and pulling down of all such idols and images as whereunto any offering had been made; and for this country (the South West) Dr Heynes, Dean of Exeter cathedral and chaplain to the King, was commissioner'. While the canons could only look on helplessly the Dean destroyed the statues in their own cathedral. At the same time as the commissioners were touring the country, proclamations were issued by the Council on 18 January and again on 6 February which caused even deeper distress and resentment among the people: candles were no longer to be blessed on Candlemas Day; all crosses and even the two lights left on the altar during Mass were to be removed along with the Easter Sepulchre; there were to be no lights and bells to accompany the priest when he carried Communion to the sick or preceded the bodies of the dead for burial in the cemetery; ashes on Ash Wednesday, palms on Palm Sunday, creeping to the Cross on Good Friday, all processions and pilgrimages were more strictly prohibited and even the distribution of blessed bread after Mass at the church door.(3) Within a matter of months the people were deprived of the ancient symbols of their faith which had been familiar to them from childhood.

The scene throughout the country, so familiar after the suppression of the monasteries, was now re-enacted: commissioners sent to enforce the Injunctions were to be seen again riding in the highways decked in the spoils of desecrated chapels, with copes for doublets or saddle-bags, and silver reliquaries hammered into sheaths for their daggers.[4]

It was for the execution of these orders from London that William Body, the Archdeacon of Cornwall, set out on a visitation of the county in the spring of 1548. Body belonged to the shadowy underworld of Thomas Cromwell's service and worked in close association with Thomas Wynter, a reputed son of Thomas Wolsey, through whose patronage he had accumulated a number of rich benefices, including the deanery of Wells and some nineteen other ecclesiastical offices. Although at one time it was thought that Wolsey would resign the see of Durham to make room for his protégé, Wynter in fact at his master's death lost all his preferments. Recovering later only the archdeaconry of Cornwall, in 1537 Wynter leased the benefice with all its properties, offices and rights to Body for a period of thirty-five years. These rights included the prebendary of Penryn and the patronage of St John's Priory at Helston in southern Cornwall.

It is not certain how much of Body's early career was known to the people of Cornwall. When in Ireland in the army on Cromwell's affairs he was believed to have brought false charges of supporting the native Irish against Leonard Grey, the Lord Deputy, which led to Grey's execution on Tower Hill in 1541. And also in Ireland he was said to have associated with the riff-raff of the camp, behaving like a stupid, unscrupulous, drunken, bragging brute.[5]

Instead of making his headquarters at Bodmin, the accepted assembly place for the county, Body chose Penryn, his prebendary, where he had a house; he then summoned to meet him there a number of parish priests and churchwardens and read out to them the Council's Injunctions. Body, however, had not reckoned on the fact that Penryn was a strong religious centre, second only to Bodmin and Launceston, with Glasney College lying just south of the town, an important centre of worship with a provost and twelve canons.

No sooner had Body finished speaking than there were loud protests. Threatening demonstrations followed. Fearing the disturbance would spread to other places Body asked the Council's instructions. On hearing his report the Council only repeated their orders, insisting that the Archdeacon should proceed on his iconoclastic mission. At once Body gave notice that all statues remaining in churches and chapels in his jurisdiction should be removed. Then on 5 April he moved on to nearby Helston, where he came up against strong resistance led by the parish priest who was known to be particularly hostile to Body.

Helston was then a populous town with a busy fish market. Until the Loe Bar formed over the mouth of the River Cober in the thirteenth century it was a much frequented port. On the west and north it was bounded by mining districts and on the north-east by farm lands. It could boast of its own saints, Gyricus and Julietta, whom the town honoured on 9 July. A stately castle indicated its importance and apart from the parish church of St Michael it still possessed a chantry close by it which had escaped the deprivations of Henry VIII, and the Priory of St John's, formerly a home for lepers, but at the time endowed by merchants as an almshouse for widows.

Along with small groups from the neighbouring hamlets of Gwennap to the north and Grade to the south the parishioners of Helston gathered to meet Body. Among them would have been members of the Cobblers Guild whose devotion to their dead members is manifest in their revised rules of 1517: making provision for their poor or unfortunate members, they established also perpetual Masses for their dead at the Guild's own altar in the parish church, gave assistance for their funerals and safeguarded as a religious duty the craft of good cobbling. These townspeople were supported by large numbers from St Keverne and Constantine: St Keverne, one of the largest and most densely populated parishes in Cornwall, was a seaport with a hardy race of fishermen; it was also the home of Michael Joseph, a blacksmith who as a young man had led a demonstration to Blackheath in protest against taxations imposed in 1497; its parish priest, Martin Geoffrey, was to play a prominent part in the disturbance following Body's arrival at Helston; at Constantine the chief landholder was William Wynslade, a young man at the time of the 1549 rebellion and one of its principal leaders.

It was a motley crowd that assembled to challenge Body - fishermen, farmers, tinners, agriculturists - some thousand men in all, armed with assorted weapons, swords, staves, sticks, hauberks, bows and arrows, but united in their purpose of preventing further sacrilege. Many in the crowd had learnt to loathe commissioners of the Crown: less than twelve years previously some of the tallest men in Cornwall (they were a tall race) had been requisitioned for the King's service against the Pilgrimage of Grace and had returned home with tales of treachery and cruel revenge.

Body was already in the church as the crowd was gathering. Taking shelter in a house said to have been at the bottom of the hill in Church Street, his refuge was immediately surrounded by the angry mob: he was dragged out, struck down and stabbed. William Kylter, a yeoman from Constantine, and Pascoe Trevian, a mariner, then came forward and despatched him. The people then moved to the market place where they were addressed by John Resseigh from Helston. Speaking on behalf of the people he declared that they 'would have all such laws as were made by the late King Henry VIII and none other until the King's majority accomplished the age of twenty-four years. And that whoso would defend Body or follow such new fashions as he did, they would punish him likewise'.

In alarm the justices the next day attempted to arrest Resseigh, but were prevented by the people, who were said now to number three thousand: their leaders threatened to take action against the officers if any of their number were brought to trial at the sessions in Helston due to open the following week. Consequently the sessions were cancelled and the crowd dispersed in triumph.

When news of the disturbance at Helston reached London the Council raised a force to restore order in the district. Launceston was reached on 17

May and a proclamation read from the castle steps offering pardon to the rioters with several named exceptions. A Grand Jury was empanelled and the trial set for 28 May. The men exempted from the pardon came mainly from the farms in the neighbourhood of Helston. William Kylter and Pascoe Trevian did not deny their guilt. The remaining twenty-six prisoners before the Bench pleaded not guilty of high treason, felony and murder: seven of these were found guilty and sentenced along with Kylter and Trevian to be hanged, drawn and quartered as traitors; an eighth, James Robert, found guilty of murder only was sentenced to be hanged. While in prison at Launceston, Kylter, a man of great strength, 'lying there in the castle green on his back threw a stone of some pounds weight over the Tower's top which leadeth to the park'.[6]

All attempts to obtain pardons or mitigation of the sentences failed. Although several members of the Council considered the sentences excessive orders were issued in June for the executions to go ahead. One execution of 'a traitor of Cornwall' was carried out on the Hoe at Plymouth, for the town accounts give details of the cost of the faggots and timber for the gallows and 'poles to put the head and quarters of the said traitor upon'.[7] Other victims were sent up to London for trial, including Fr Martin Geoffrey, the parish priest of St Keverne: he was hanged, drawn and quartered at Smithfield on 7 June 1548; five of the others sent up to the capital were pardoned.

2. THE FAITH IN CORNWALL

The Helston riot and the brutal executions that followed left a smouldering resentment throughout the county. Silently disaffection spread and it seemed not impossible that a second Pilgrimage of Grace would begin in the west.

Later in the same year and well into 1549 there were disturbances throughout the length of the kingdom, from Sussex, Hampshire, Surrey and Kent through Oxfordshire to Somerset and Wiltshire. In Norfolk also there was a threatened rising. Partly religious, partly agrarian in origin they were sporadic, short-lived, uncoordinated and with the exception of Norfolk lacking an effective leader. Undoubtedly the commons were suffering: rents had increased and in places had soared since the transfer of monastic estates to lay owners who now fixed wages to suit their pleasure. In retrospect the monks appeared compassionate landlords; they had also been generous in their distribution of alms on which the poor now more than ever depended. With these hardships went a debasement of the coinage and mounting inflation.

The commons had been led to believe that with the application of monastic funds to the Treasury taxes would be reduced: in fact taxes had either increased or remained the same. The men at court down to the minor officials had all been enriched with the spoils of the monastic houses and were considered, with good reason, to have a vested interest in advancing the religious changes. Lord Russell, for instance, who was to lead the Government forces against the Rising in the west, was no more than a small landowner when he began his career in the royal service: he had possessed no estates in Devon or Cornwall until Henry VIII on 4 July 1539 granted him the Cistercian monastery of Dunkeswell and the site of the rich abbey of Tavistock, along with the greater part of its possessions, which included the town itself, and more than thirty manors, a house in Exeter, estates in Buckinghamshire and Somerset and some properties formerly owned by St Albans Abbey.

Six years later, when war with France made it necessary to strengthen the western defences, Henry made him Lieutenant of Devon and Cornwall, with orders to raise levies, impress seamen and maintain internal order. Cornishmen and perhaps still more the people of Devon had good grounds for detesting him because the church at Tavistock had contained the shrine of its patron, St Rumon, which had been duly dismantled, its gold, silver and jewelled ornaments sent to the Tower and the remains of the saint desecrated. The shrine had been well frequented for it lay across the border between the two counties on a point directly in line with the main road from Bodmin to Liskeard. With the end of the abbey went the abolition of the three day festival in honour of the saint from the vigil on the 29 August.

In Devon and Cornwall agrarian discontent was less acute than in other parts of England and was scarcely a factor contributing to the rebellion of 1549. The enclosure of common land, an almost universal cause of distress, hardly affected Cornwall, a fact that is borne out by the very small number of cases that came from the county to the Court of Requests: land there which the tinners could not use had long since been given over to pasture.

After the disturbances in Helston the Council became aware of the danger of more widespread disturbances in the South West, putting the blame on the priests who with 'a develish mind and intent' were inciting the people 'as well in confession as otherwise to disobedience and stubbornness against his Majesty's godly proceedings'.[1] All preaching was forbidden in parish churches except under special licence; instead priests were compelled to read from the book of Homilies compiled by Cranmer and published in July 1547.

The roots of the people's devotion went deep. Foreign travellers were impressed by the piety of the commons, by their attendance at Mass every day, the women carrying rosaries in their hand and any who could read taking with them the office of Our Lady which they would recite in church with a companion in a low voice.[2] This attachment to weekday Mass is borne out by the frequent requests of the gentry to keep in their homes an altar and a priest to serve it and also by Cranmer himself who deprecated the desire of 'lewd' lay people to see the Host at least once a day. In addition the guilds everywhere made arrangements for several daily Masses in their parish churches. It is thought that most lay people attended at least one weekday Mass which was usually celebrated not at the back of the rood screen but at a side altar with the people kneeling close to the priest.[3]

Cornwall had its own good reasons for adhering to the old faith. It was the country of countless saints that went back in folk memory to Celtic times before Christianity took root in the rest of the island: the rebellion there to retain the ancient faith was a spontaneous expression of the people's piety without any previous plot or planning. The Romans had never penetrated beyond Exeter, leaving Cornwall a foreign country with close ties to Brittany where the same language was spoken and religious devotion expressed in the same forms. Up to the eve of the Reformation Cornishmen, like the Bretons across the Channel, were erecting crosses on the country roads at which peasants carrying their dead for burial took a rest and pious folk passing on the road stopped to say a prayer. On the wind-swept moors there were similar crosses to guide travellers on their way. The holy wells drew simple people seeking a cure for one ailment or another. The waters of St Cadoc's near Padstow were thought to expel venomous diseases and worms from the stomach, while Cornishmen crossed to Brittany to be cured of deafness at the tomb of St Mawes.

But the two peoples had also their saints in common, honouring them with the same prayers on the same day. Only seventy years before the Rising, William, a monk of Worcester, made notes of their feast-days and of the rites celebrated in honour of each of them - Cadoc, Piran, Geroe and innumerable others. In every town named after a hermit or monk there was a Mass and fair to commemorate its patron and his legend or history was made familiar to the townspeople in the stone carvings and in the stained glass windows of their church. At St Neot stained glass windows which have survived the iconoclasm were erected as late as 1529 in honour of their saint, a dwarf no more than fifteen inches high who used to stand in the water up to his neck reciting the Book of Psalms.

The legends of the saints were also made familiar to the people through religious plays such as the drama based on the life of St Meriadec, the patron of Camborne. While his life story unfolds on the stage the saint pauses to explain the doctrine of the virgin birth. Other plays surviving from that period were for more general instruction in the doctrines of the faith: their popularity is testified to by the large earthen amphitheatres, as for instance at St Just-in-Penwith, constructed in the open with a capacity for some two thousand spectators. Comic interludes and spectacular stage effects such as earthquakes, eclipses and the crossing of the Red Sea helped to attract large audiences.

With the abolition of the festivals in honour of the saints the people were deprived both of their plays and of their religious instruction. Disallowed by Henry VIII, these customs were now condemned by the Council as superstitious. The people of St Keverne (men from the town had been very active in the Helston riot and had suffered for it) had in the past petitioned Henry VIII for permission to hold their saint's day 'solemnly as they were wont to do'. The King had consented, but the custom was nevertheless suppressed in the new reign.

A special case was that of St Petroc, always Cornwall's favourite saint, a Celtic monk who, after founding several monasteries, had lived for a time as a hermit on Bodmin moor, where he was followed by twelve disciples. Until its suppression in 1530, his shrine in Bodmin had been the focus of Cornish piety. He had been buried first at Padstow (Petroc's church), but his tomb there had been exposed to the raids, first of the Saxon, then later of the Danish, pirates. When the monks moved for protection to Bodmin they brought the saint's body with them. From 905 the church there, thanks to St Petroc, became the episcopal see of Cornwall until 981, when it was burnt down by the Danes and the see transferred to St Germans. The remains of the saint, however, were retained at Bodmin. Stolen and taken in 1180 to the abbey of St Mein in Brittany, they were returned on the orders of Henry II in a painted ivory casket: a few bones, some hair and pieces of his clothing had previously, in the tenth century, been presented to the monastery of St Peter in Exeter by Athelstan, King of the West Saxons.

Well into the sixteenth century pilgrims from Brittany, which became part of France only in 1492, visited Petroc's shrine while others constituted a sizeable percentage of the population of the Cornish towns. Mainly devout fishermen or labourers they were scarcely regarded as foreigners. In 1530 John Leland in his tour of the country remarked on the crowd of small vessels that put into Padstow to exchange goods from Brittany with fish from the Cornishmen. In 1538 a visiting Breton priest accused of spreading disaffection in the South West was brought before the Justice, Sir Thomas Dennis, who was later active in suppressing the rebellion, and imprisoned by him in Exeter gaol: his case was considered grave enough to be brought to the attention of the Privy Council. Six years later, in 1544, for instance, there were fourteen Breton families, perhaps fifty persons, living at Constantine, a town involved in the Helston riot: among those arrested at the time were Laurence Breton and Michael Vian Breton; and in the following year Bretons from the

South West contributed their quota, which included their chief gunner, to the rebel forces. Further west, at Penwith, Bretons formed ten per cent of the population.

Thanks to St Petroc, Bodmin, where the rebels mustered on the eve of the rebellion, became the traditional assembly place for Cornishmen and a focus of religious worship comparable to the shrine of St Thomas at Canterbury. At the beginning of the sixteenth century apart from the parish church it had a Priory and no less than thirteen chapels or chantries and three hospitals, St George's and St Anthony's in the town and St Lawrence's outside. There were also more than forty guilds in the town, all of them founded in part at least for a religious purpose; and it was through them that money was raised for schools, hospitals and the maintenance of the fabric of the churches.

While murmurings continued against the iconoclastic proclamations of the Council, Cranmer, now free of all ties that bound him to the old religion, was busy preparing the way for the service that would replace the Mass. A preparatory step was taken on 8 May 1548 when his new Order of Service was introduced by Proclamation and appointed to come into force at Easter the following year. The Service substituted English for Latin in the prayers before Communion: this in itself was not an innovation that disturbed the people, who seldom received the Sacrament except at Easter. On the other hand it did nothing to dispel the anxiety of the people who feared that further changes were about to follow.

Their fears were soon justified. Not long after Easter in St Paul's cathedral and in some other

London churches the entire Mass, together with Matins and Evensong, was allowed in English and, in addition, the people were encouraged not to restrict their reception of Communion to Easter. That autumn Cranmer led the bishops assembled at Windsor in a discussion of a draft Prayer Book to replace the Missal. From the debates that followed in the House of Lords it is difficult to determine the Archbishop's exact theological position: although it appeared to be constantly changing at the time of the discussions, it would seem not to have been far from that of the Swiss Reformer, Ulrich Zwingli, who rejected the sacrifice of the Mass and the invocation of the saints

Moreover, while Cranmer was working on the new Service, the Protestant Reformer, John a Lasco (or Laski), whose sympathies were with the extreme form of Calvinism, visited England at the Archbishop's invitation: although the avowed purpose of his visit was to advise Cranmer on reforms there is no means of gauging the extent of his influence. However, no matter what lay at the back of Cranmer's mind or whatever part might have been played by Lasco, there is no doubt that the new form of worship in meaning and content was totally different from the old Eucharistic faith.

The Prayer Book passed both Houses of Parliament on 21 January 1549. On 4 March it received royal assent. Henceforth a cleric refusing to use the Book was fined the yield of his benefice for one year; for the second offence he would lose for his lifetime all his benefices and be imprisoned for a year; for the third it was life imprisonment. As for laymen, anyone attacking the Book or procuring a cleric to use any other form of worship would suffer a rising scale of fines, losing all his possessions on the third offence.

The Prayer Book has been described as a masterpiece of compromise and ambiguity: while it did not specifically deny Catholic doctrine it could be interpreted in a sense acceptable to the Reformers.[4] It was also a great work of simplification and transformation. The shape of the Mass was retained but the doctrine that each Mass was a sacrifice was eliminated, as well as any notion of change in the bread and wine at the consecration. The emphasis was shifted from a sacrificial offering to a memorial service of thanksgiving. Everywhere, also, the Prayer Book changed the ancient sacramental rituals and in some places by altering the rubrics or the directives for the priest left no doubt that its intention was to introduce the new doctrines which Cranmer and his associates undoubtedly held. The anointing with the oil of catechumens was omitted from baptism and also the oil of chrism from confirmation; in funerals incense and holy water were done away with, and there was to be no blessing of the grave or prayer for the repose of the souls of the dead person; Extreme Unction was presented not as a sacrament in its own right but as an optional devotion in the visitation of the sick by the priest. It was the same with the sacrament of Penance; and there was not even a suggestion that Christian marriage was a sacrament.

By eliminating the elevation of the Host Cranmer did away with the popular focus of Eucharistic worship. Most of the feasts of the liturgical year were removed from the calendar; only Christmas, Easter and Whitsun, shorn of their octaves, remained, along with days in honour of John the

Baptist, the Apostles, Evangelists and Mary Magdalene. All but one of the feasts of Our Lady were abolished, including the Assumption, that had been longer in the calendar of England than in any country in the west. All votive Masses which helped to draw the people to church on weekdays were removed without exception.

But the book had two advantages which later came to be valued by the Reformed Church in England. In the first place, the Mass, Matins and all the sacramental Rites were included in a single book; and, secondly, the translation, often rather loose, was in incomparable English that was to exercise such a spell over the minds of the people in the centuries to follow. There is no indication, however, that Cranmer's exquisite prose captivated those who in his own century listened under compulsion to its magical rhythms. While in his letters, disputations and reports, both in English and Latin, Cranmer wrote in turgid, commonplace and diffuse language, he toiled over every phrase and cadence of the Prayer Book with unmatched skill. On the other hand, the change to English made superfluous the entire musical riches of the medieval English church.

To the common people, however, what really mattered was that everything was now in English. This more than any alteration or omission roused their suspicions. They were instinctively aware that the old Latin was the surest safeguard of orthodoxy. Moreover, at one stroke they had been deprived of the mysticism and mystery that enveloped their lives. In spite of Cranmer's avowed purpose to keep something of the form of the old Mass it is not difficult to appreciate the resentment of the commons at the forthcoming feast of Whitsun, when the solemn Mass was reduced to a lifeless dialogue between the parish priest and the sexton. In Cornwall the commons knew their way about the Latin Mass and understood many of its phrases. Now it was in a foreign tongue which far from all the people understood.

3. THE BODMIN RISING

Unlike the riot at Helston there was no particular incident that sparked off the disturbance at Bodmin, the cradle of the rebellion in the west. Its cause, however, is clear from the petition the Cornishmen presented to the Council in the form of Articles, all but one of which demanded the return of the old religious practices and beliefs of the commons. No sooner kindled than the flame of revolt spread in the space of a week from one end of the peninsula to the other, a spontaneous outbreak starting with ordinary folk and soon joined by several well-connected men of wealth and position.

The first stirrings of the Rising occurred on 6 June, the first anniversary of the execution at Smithfield of Fr Martin Geoffrey, the parish priest of St Keverne's: the memory of his brutal death and of the repressive measures that followed it were still very fresh in Cornwall. The anniversary happened to occur two days before the feast of Pentecost, when the new service replacing the old Mass was to be introduced in all churches throughout the country. In the course of the months since the executions of the previous year the commissioners whose task it was to make a survey of church goods had descended on Bodmin where the furnishings of the Priory church had been removed, including chalices, censers, crosses, vestments of silver damask, velvet and satin of Bruges and all Mass books; only the bones of St Petroc in the painted ivory casket had been saved from the commissioners and stowed away in secret. It had been the same story at Liskeard and in all places where records survive.

Protector Somerset and the Council could hardly have chosen a worse time for the compulsory introduction of Cranmer's Prayer Book: war was on the point of breaking out against both France and Scotland; there was a widespread agrarian crisis; there were disturbances close at hand in Hertfordshire, while at the same time there were rumours of risings in Gloucester, Worcester, Rutland, Norfolk and Suffolk. But what alarmed Council most was the report that the gentlemen of Cornwall had joined the priests and commons. Rightly convinced that religion was the root cause of the Rising, the Government's first reaction was to despatch Myles Coverdale, who had recently returned from Tubingen, to reconcile the people to the changes in religion: a former priest and intimate of Cranmer, he was considered the most effective preacher of the day. He left London on 15 June, a week after the first assembly of the rebels at Bodmin. John Hooker, the Protestant historian of the rebellion, who was living in Exeter at the time, states unequivocally that the cause of the rebellion was 'only concerning religion which then by Act of Parliament was reformed'.[1] The new sheep tax which the government had imposed was undoubtedly resented, but the request for its abolition which was added to the demands of the rebels did not alter the purely religious character of the Rebellion.

Among those who joined the commons of Cornwall were several gentlemen with years of experience in warfare abroad. Their overall commander, Humphry Arundell of Helland, some five miles from Bodmin, was to prove a skilled tactician. Thirty-six years old at the time, he was a scion of the Arundells of Lanherne, which from the middle of the thirteenth century had been prominent in the civic and ecclesiastical affairs of Cornwall: early in the sixteenth century John Arundell had been Dean of Exeter and later Bishop of Lichfield and finally of Exeter in 1502; more recently Sir Thomas had served as a commissioner for the suppression of the monasteries; a younger brother of the same house, Sir John, had married a sister of Queen Catherine Howard and on the accession of Edward VI had been made a Privy Councillor.

Through his mother, Joan, the heiress of Humphry Calwodley of Calwoodleigh in Devon, Humphry Arundell had inherited large estates across the county border, an association with Devon made him an acceptable leader when the rebels of the two counties joined forces at Crediton. Humphry's name appears among the men enlisted for war against France, to which he brought ten footmen. A contemporary author calls him a 'man well esteemed for his military services'.[2] There is evidence that he was a somewhat turbulent landowner, but nevertheless he had been a member of the Grand Jury for the trial of the Helston rioters in the year before the Rising. He is described also as the Governor or Captain of the Mount or Mount St Michael in southern Cornwall: the peninsula had once belonged to Sion Abbey and may well have been granted to him on the Dissolution of the monastic houses; five or six soldiers formed its garrison against a possible French landing and it is likely that Humphry had been designated as their commander.

With Humphry Arundell was John Wynslade who, like Humphry, held land in both counties. At Tregarrick, his main residence, he was said to keep 'great hospitality'. His wife Jane was the daughter of Sir John Trelawney of Menheniot, where the church dedicated to St Neot contains numerous monuments to the family. Their son William also took a very active part in the rebellion.

The Wynslade family were Esquires of the White Spurs, a rare distinction shared in the West Country only with the Coplestones of Lamerton in Devon: the title denotes military prowess, which was far from lacking among the rebels. With the Wynslades was John Bury, described as the 'chief captain of all saving one', who had estates scattered over the country at Hartland, Ugborough, Tavistock, Plympton and elsewhere: he was a formidable soldier like another rebel gentleman, Robert Smyth of Tregonack in St Germans, who was to lead the charge of the rebels in the first engagement with the government forces at Fenny Bridges near Honiton. A close neighbour of Humphry Arundell, he resided in his wife's home at Blisland where a number of their retainers joined the rebel forces. But almost as important as Arundell in the reckoning of the government was Sir Thomas Pomeroy. Now forty-six years old, he had been a commander under Henry VIII in the French wars.

These men, along with an unidentified William Fortescue from a well-known Devon family, represented the gentry of Devon and Cornwall. Since there are virtually no documents extant from the rebel camp, other gentlemen may have fought with them.

Serving under these leaders were men from all strata of society: the mayors of Torrington and Bodmin, tailors, fishermen, as well as merchants from Exeter. The clergy accompanied them in large numbers, including men of equal calibre to Richard Crispyn and John Moreman, who, in 1547, had been imprisoned in the Tower for preaching Romish doctrines. Crispyn, a canon of Exeter cathedral and formerly a Fellow of Oriel College and chaplain to the Marquis of Exeter, had been rector of Harbeton in Devon; his fellow prisoner, John Moreman, had been Dean of Exeter College, Oxford, and Principal of Hart Hall. At Menheniot, the home of the Trelawneys, he had devoted himself to the 'honourable fatigue of instructing youth in school learning'.[3] When at Oxford he had opposed the divorce proceedings of Henry VIII and on coming to Menheniot he had shown himself well in advance of his time, instructing his parishioners to recite the Our Father, the Creed and the Commandments in English. Priests of this type joining the rebels were to suffer cruelly, men like the Rector of Crede, the Vicars of St Clare, St Uny and, the best known of them, the Vicar of Poundstock, as well as numerous others who had 'commanded the people to stick to their idolatry'.[4]

Humphry Arundell was at his house in Helland, at the time of the gathering there. In the account of the events he gave at his trial he pleaded that he had become the reluctant leader of the rebels, claiming that while at home with his wife a Bodmin rebel had come petitioning him to join their assembly, and that when he refused others had come and taken him away by force; then, again, according to his account, he wrote to the sheriff, Sir Hugh Trevanion, enquiring what he should do and was advised 'to tarry with the rebels' so that 'he could mitigate their outrageous doings'.

Whether true or not Arundell accepted their leadership. The crowd then moved out of Bodmin through the lanes and along the high road to the old British fortification of Castle Kynock, half a mile to the south west. There Arundell was appointed General. Under his command the rebel forces were divided into detachments in military fashion under colonels, majors and captains; several priests, vicars and curates were given positions of responsibility. Then plans were discussed.

To secure his rear before advancing towards London Arundell despatched a party of horse to besiege the Mount: they were mainly Arundell's own men who were familiar with the place. No doubt their mounts were the hardy, coarsely-fed Cornish horses, low in stature, quick in travel and eminently serviceable in rough and hilly country; some footmen went with them. Arundell realised that it would always be possible for a government force to be landed in small boats under the Mount in his rear, though the more immediate danger was from the Protestant gentlemen of the county who had gathered there for safety during the disturbance at Bodmin.

Approaching the Mount at low tide the rebels carried in front of them great trusses of hay to deaden the enemy's fire, 'after which they (the defenders) could make but slender resistance, for no sooner should one within peep out his head over those enflanking walls but he became an open mark to a whole shower of arrows.[5]

The success at the Mount brought further crowds to the rebel cause. Some six thousand people greeted the return of the troop to Bodmin, such a formidable gathering that the sheriff of Cornwall,

John Milton, was incapable of taking any action
against them.

Left to themselves the rebels drew up a
manifesto declaring the justice of their demands,
which they hammered out in eight Articles and
despatched to the King. The exact contents of the
Articles can only be inferred from Somerset's reply:
apart possibly from a request for relief from the sheep
tax they were wholly concerned with religion. They
asked that curates should not be restricted to
administering baptism only on Sundays and feast-
days, as the rubric laid down, but be ready to baptise
every day of the week, a significant demand in an age
when one baby in ten died in its first year of life,
many on the day it was born and many more in its
first week. Confirmation should also be more
available and bishops should confirm children
whenever they resorted to them; Mass should be
celebrated with only the priest communicating; the
sacrament should be reserved in churches; holy bread
and water was to be distributed at the church door;
Mass was to be in Latin, for the Cornishmen did not
understand English, and it was to be said or sung in
the choir and not set forth in front of the people 'like a
Christmas play'. In addition, the clergy should not be
permitted to marry and the Six Articles of religion set
forth by the late King which had been repealed in the
first Parliament of the new reign should continue in
force until his son King Edward came of age. In
conclusion 'they prayed God save the King, as they
were his (men) both body and soul'.

This conclusion to the Articles was no hollow
expression of loyalty to the Crown. At this time and
throughout earlier centuries it was commonly

accepted that when a tyrant overrode the welfare of his people it was their legitimate right to take up arms against him with the purpose of making him change his mind or his ministers: this right was acknowledged to be implicit in the coronation service in which it was accepted that the King ruled by the sufferance of his people.

But, for the legitimacy of a rising, representatives of the nobility had to be involved: it was not sufficient for the common people to go it alone. In Cornwall, however, there were virtually no resident nobility: heiresses had for a long time been marrying outside the county, taking with them their 'inhabitance together with their inheritance'.[6] Added to this was a reluctance to live so far from the centre of affairs. A number of families like the Courtenays, de Veres and Spencers possessed estates in Cornwall but did not reside there; and there were other nobles who were not anxious to live in the shadow of the royal Duchy. Nevertheless, if allowance is made for the Protestants, like the Grenvilles, among the Cornish gentry who had a vested landed interest in the reformed religion, the gentlemen of Cornwall were more than sufficiently represented to meet the requirement for a legitimate rising.

More than this, the Western rebels in drawing up their Articles considered themselves still further justified because all that they substantially demanded was that the will of the late King should be respected until his son became of age.

While these demands were despatched to London there was a disturbance across the county border that was to increase the alarm of the Council.

4. WHITSUN AT SAMPFORD COURTENAY

On 8 June, Whit Sunday that year, two days after the first stirring in Bodmin, an excited, motley crowd, rather more numerous than usual, made its way through the narrow, deep Devonshire lanes to the church of St Andrew in Sampford Courtenay, a small village in mid Devon on the fringe of Dartmoor. Although the church lay in a hollow, its tower, one of the most majestic in the county, could be seen from many parts of the parish.

It was the day appointed by the Council for the compulsory introduction of the new service devised mainly by Archbishop Cranmer to replace the old Mass. The parish priest, Fr William Harper, a man of seventy, no longer wearing the rich embroidered red chasuble, read dutifully from the Book of Common Prayer. This was not the solemn Whitsun Mass for which the people had been accustomed to prepare by a day of fasting. There was no procession inside the church in which the congregation participated, as the priest, to the accompaniment of plainchant, blessed the side altars and the people; there were no lights on the altar or on the rood screen or anywhere in the church, and no elevation of the Host which was the focal expression of the community's worship. The congregation was restive. Harangued outside the church after the service by its leading members it was agreed that when they met the next day for the customary Mass to inaugurate the Whitsun festival they would have no more of the new form of worship.

The congregation was even larger on the Monday. As the priest came from his house down the path to the church, Thomas Underhill, a tailor, and his friend, William Segar, a labourer, blocked his way, demanding to know whether he intended to offer Mass or to read the new service.

'In obedience to the law I must use the new service book,' Fr Harper answered.

'That indeed you will not do,' he was told abruptly. 'We will stand by the laws and ordinances touching Christian religion as were appointed by King Henry (God rest his soul) until the King's Majesty that now is reaches the age of twenty-four years, for so his father appointed it.'

There was a roar of applause. The crowd clapped their approval. In the words of Hooker, the priest was forced to put on 'his old Popish attire' and say the Mass in Latin 'as in past times accustomed'.[1]

Since it was a holiday, news of events at Sampford Courtenay spread rapidly to neighbouring parishes 'as a cloud carried by a violent wind and as a thunder clap sounding at one instant throughout the whole country.'[2] Around every church in the district people were gathering for their Whitsun ale: according to the time-honoured custom two churchwardens, after taking a collection from the parishioners, shared the responsibility of brewing the ale and baking the cakes to accompany it. At Sampford Courtenay, as elsewhere, people gathered after Mass in the church house, several of them adding 'some petty portion to the stock'. As neighbouring parishes visited one another to sample their ale the disturbance across the border at Bodmin was the main subject of their conversation. The celebrations continued throughout the afternoon, which was 'consumed in such exercises as old and young folk (having leisure) do accustomably wear out the time withal'.[3] The people were in a triumphant as well as a festive mood. Archery competitions were organised (Robert Bone was known to be able to shoot a little bird perched on a cow's back) and a form of hurling in which two bushes eight or ten feet apart marked the goals and an 'indifferent' judge acted as umpire: they hurled the ball from man to man, no two players setting on one man at the same time.[4]

These games continued into the evening, other parishes joining in. It was a time of 'Christian love, the compounding of controversies, the appeasing of quarrels, raising a store (fund) which might be converted to good and godly uses as relieving all sorts of poor people, repairing of churches, building of bridges, and amending highways, and partly, for the Prince's service, by defraying at an instance such rates and taxes as the magistrate imposes for the defence of the country'.[5]

Meanwhile, speeches continued against the innovations in religion, becoming more defiant and inflammatory as the evening wore on. Local justices, led by Sir Hugh Pollard and Anthony Harvey, after providing themselves with an escort, hurried to the village to restore the King's peace. Warned of their approach the leading parishioners consulted together, 'so addicted and wholly bent on their follies', wrote Hooker, 'that they fully resolved themselves willingly to maintain what naughtily they had begun.'[6] When the justices arrived they were not permitted to parley until they had left their armed escort.

Unwilling to use force, possibly out of sympathy with the rioters, the justices retired. It was then that a respected franklin from a neighbouring parish, William Hellyons, urged the people to renounce their rebellion, but he only made them bolder. The poor man was carried off a prisoner to the church house 'where he so earnestly reproved them for their disobedience ... that they fell in a rage with him, and not only with evil words reviled him, but also, as he was going out of the church house and going down the stairs, one of them named Lithibridge, with a bill struck him in the neck and immediately, notwithstanding his pitiful requests and lamentations, a number of the rest fell on him and slew him and cut him in small pieces'.[7]

This was the first blood shed in the rebellion. The crowd no doubt realised that their purpose would best be achieved if they united with the Cornish rebels. The people from Sampford Courtenay, therefore, with men from the neighbouring parishes made for Crediton which the advance contingents of Arundell's army were now approaching.

Even before his success at the Mount, Arundell had begun his march towards London, determined to enforce the just demands of the commons and obtain security for their fulfilment: he was not prepared to be fobbed off with condescending promises in the King's name which the government had no intention of honouring as had happened in the Pilgrimage of Grace in the previous reign. Among Arundell's troops were the famous Cornish archers, who at the time had been impressed to march north against the pilgrims.

Banners were unfurled, including that of the Five Wounds to which the northerners had rallied thirteen years earlier: it was the emblem of the devotion popular throughout England to the Wounds of the suffering Christ and was familiar to the people not only through its special office and Mass for the relief of the poor and distressed, but through the practice of acts of charity done in multiples of five on Fridays of the week and especially on Good Friday; by the fifteenth century the insignia of the Five Wounds had become the popular expression of the people's loyalty to the whole Catholic belief and practice. Behind the banner the pyx, which customarily hung over the altar and contained the Sacrament, was carried by a priest.

It was far from a mob brandishing pitchforks and farm instruments that set out from Bodmin: as the musters of 1522 show, the Cornish peasants were in possession of a striking armoury of weapons. They marched in rough military formation carrying, as Hooker writes, 'swords, shields, clubs, cannons, halberts, lances and other arms, offensive and defensive'.[8] Their most formidable weapon was their bow: when, after the engagement on Blackheath in 1497, the Englishmen cleared the field they were astonished to discover that the Cornish bow was a good six inches longer than theirs. As most of Cornwall was involved in the Rising it is reckoned that between two and three thousand men would probably have followed Arundell, most of them infantry in their full harness: this consisted of a helmet, a gorget to guard the throat, a coat of leather or canvas with small metal plates sewn into it, and splints, except in the case of archers, to protect the forearm. Probably one in three were bowmen, the greater part of the remainder carried a bill six feet long that could be used as a spear or axe, a weapon designed for close-in fighting.[9] Ahead was borne the pyx containing the consecrated Host 'under a canopy with crosses, banners, candlesticks, holy bread and water', an old time Corpus Christi procession such as had been held in the parishes of England since the thirteenth century, which according to the indictment of the leading rebels was intended 'to defend them from the devils and the adverse power'.[10]

The marchers set much reliance on the unpopularity of the Protector Somerset and on the help they were likely to receive from other counties on their route that shared their grievances. Confident of success and full of faith they sang songs and hymns as they made their way over the trackless wastes of Bodmin moor and then across the Tamar at Polson Bridge into Devon. On their way a detachment under Robert Smyth, whose ancestral home was at St Germans, was sent south to Plymouth: he followed the old road through Liskeard and Menheniot, whose Rector was still a prisoner in the Tower, to the city boundary. Their progress, however, was checked by Richard Grenville, the father of the Elizabethan mariner, who twelve months earlier had sat in judgement on the Helston rioters as head of a specially appointed commission. Grenville and his lady had sought refuge in Trematon Castle, their fortified home where they were duly besieged. More impressive than Launceston, the castle commanded views towards Hamoaze and the Sound: the tall walls of its inner bailey remain today as an indication of its strength at the time. Luring Grenville to the gatehouse for a parley, the rebels slipped between him and his home. The castle surrendered and the rebels pushed on the few miles to Plymouth. The city yielded without a fight, but the castle held out. With fresh recruits, and no doubt supplies of ordnance,

Smyth rejoined the main body by way of Tavistock and Launceston, then followed the swelling army across Dartmoor to Crediton.

Crediton was a prosperous town that could sustain Arundell's forces, its wealth based on a thriving woollen industry on which merchants had made their fortunes and like the Northcotes were to found landed families. Close to the town was Yewton Arundell, a house belonging to Humphry, which he straightway made his headquarters.

The Council did not expect the Prayer Book to be received without protest. On the Monday of the Samford Courtenay riot the Protector Somerset had in fact sent letters to the Marquis of Dorset and to the Earl of Huntingdon, warning them against 'sundry lewd persons who at the instigation of seditious priests and other evil persons' might seek to stir up the people: if such attempts were made they were to be suppressed instantly.[11]

Accordingly, when reports of the insurrection in Devon and Cornwall reached London the majority in the Council favoured instant repressive measures. Sir William Paget, the leading Councillor advocating stern treatment, was then on an embassy abroad: Paget had stood high in favour of the old King and on his death had convened the Council and had obtained their agreement to the appointment of Somerset as Protector and Regent, setting aside any claim of Princess Mary to the position. He now urged Somerset, who had proved himself a brilliant soldier in Scotland, to put himself at the head of four thousand Almayn (German) mercenaries then idle at Calais, then send for Lord Ferris and Sir William Herbert to bring horsemen from Wales and for the

Earl of Shrewsbury to join them. 'Should the rebels come peaceably to justice,' he advised Somerset, 'let six be hanged of the ripest of them without redemptions, the rest to remain in prison'. As for the other chief rebels, they should be taken from their wives to be soldiers in Boulogne or in the north.[12] Somerset, however, continued to urge restraint. As a compromise it was agreed that Sir Peter Carew, who had been appointed sheriff of Devonshire in the last year of Henry's reign and had his seat at Mohun's Ottery close to Exeter, and his uncle, Sir Gawen, owner of Tiverton Castle, should be sent letters authorising them to use all means and ways 'for the appeasing of this rebellion; quieting the people and pacifying the country; and to cause every man to return quietly to his home and to refer the causes of their grief and complaints, if they had any, to the King and Council.'[13]

Sir Peter, a soldier of fortune, undoubtedly possessed the necessary military skill to suppress any rising if he was given sufficient forces: 'sharp was his understanding,' writes Hooker, who knew him intimately, 'pithy were his arguments and deep was his judgement ... for besides his advice and counsel, ready in all matters, such was his skill and experience in martial affairs that he could pitch a camp, martial a field, set, array and order the battle with such wisdom, dexterity and policy as should be to the best advantage and safeguard of the army and the most annoyance to the enemy.'[14]

Peter's reputation for ruthlessness satisfied the more uncomprising members of the Council. As a 'perte and forward youth' he had played truant at the grammar school in Exeter, run away from Dean

Collet's new and fashionable establishment of St Paul's in London and, being 'more desirous of liberty than learning', he had crossed to France and served as a nobleman's lackey, stableman and finally as his valet. Entering the army of Francis I, the King of France, he had taken part in the great battle of Pavia in 1525, and had then gone over to the camp of Charles V. Later, while he was in the service of Philibert de Chalons he was sent over on business to the court of Henry VIII. Although only sixteen at the time he advanced rapidly. Remaining at the English court as a gentleman of the Privy Chamber he was sent to escort Anne of Cleves to England; then in 1544, when war broke out with France, he joined the campaign with a hundred foot. In 1545 he had distinguished himself in command of a warship, while his elder brother captained the ill-fated Mary Rose. When he received the summons to handle the disturbance at Sampford Courtenay he was at the home of his recently married wife in Lincolnshire.

Sir Gawen was even less likely than his nephew to recommend himself as a mediator to the enraged commons of Sampford Courtenay. In 1540 he had acquired the lease of the Priory at Launceston, with its numerous dependencies, but in spite of representations made in London he had refused to fulfil his obligation of maintaining curates in the churches included in the grant. Added to this, in the year before the Rising he had incurred the odium of the people as a commissioner for the suppression of the chantries.

On 20 June, however, twelve days after the riot at Sampford Courtenay, Somerset was still advocating leniency towards 'them that would not read the book of services', ordering the justices and other gentlemen of Devonshire to accept that the rebels had acted 'rather out of ignorance than of malice and at the motion of some light and naughty persons than of any evil will that our loving subjects' bore towards him or the realm:[15] the offenders were not to be 'troubled or vexed for any such offence hereafter' so long as they behaved as loving and obedient subjects.

This was precisely how the rebels regarded themselves, insisting as they did that the will of the late King should be respected.

5. THE FIRST ENCOUNTERS

On reaching Exeter the two Carews summoned the sheriffs and justices of the peace to a conference. It was there decided that they should both be given an escort and ride to Crediton, five miles away, and hold a parley with the rebels who had now joined forces there. News of the appointment of Sir Peter Carew, however, had only increased the commons' determination 'to maintain their cause ... and make themselves strong with such armour and furniture as they had'.[1]

The rebels had not been idle. Crediton was now an entrenched camp and the highway from Exeter where it crossed the River Clyst at the approach to the town was blocked by a rampart, with a barn on each side which had been converted into forts, their walls pierced with apertures and manned by picked archers. The Carews' mounted vanguard unable to advance turned back. After a short discussion it was decided to approach the rebels on foot, thinking that in this way they would not be obstructed. The Carews were mistaken: they were unable to get near the rampart and their request for a parley was rejected. 'Sir Peter, however, accustomed to cross swords with the French chivalry, was not to be daunted by village churls'.[2] He charged the rampart, only to be driven back with some losses. But in the assault a servant of Sir Hugh Pollard, the justice of the peace who earlier in the month had gone to parley with the rioters at Sampford Courtenay, set one of the barns on fire. Evacuating both barns in panic the defenders fled. Carew's men entered the town, but only to find it deserted apart from a few old people.

As there was no one with whom he could parley and as he had insufficient men to hold the town Sir Peter returned to Exeter: he had done nothing to quell the commons: he had learned, however, that the Rising was more serious than the Council had given him to believe and that a considerable force would be needed to suppress it.

Meanwhile the rumour spread through the countryside that the barns had been deliberately set on fire: such an allegedly cruel action 'carried and blasted through the countryside' convinced the commons that the Carews were bent to 'overrun, spoil and destroy them'.(3) Straightaway they set about entrenching the highways, throwing up ramparts, felling trees and fortifying villages.

Among the places that raised defences was the small village of Clyst St Mary, less than three miles from Exeter. It happened that Walter Raleigh, a Devonshire gentleman and father of the naval commander, riding out to Exeter from his home at Hayes Barton in the parish of East Budleigh overtook an old woman on her way to church at Clyst: she was carrying her rosary beads, a sure indication that she adhered to the old Catholic practices. Reprimanded and threatened by Raleigh with the penalties of the law she took to her heels, burst into the church, where the parishioners were celebrating a holy day, and in an excited torrent of words led the worshippers to believe that Raleigh had warned her that unless she threw away her rosary he and his men would return, burn down the village and destroy their homes. At once the parishioners fortified the bridge which carried the Exeter road over the river Clyst at the approach to the village, felled some trees, laid them

across the road and placed on the bridge some
ordnance taken from the nearby naval base at
Topsham. At the same time some of the congregation
set out in pursuit of Raleigh and caught up with him
before he could reach Exeter: 'they were in such a
coler ... that if he had not shifted himself into the
chapel there and had been rescued by certain mariners
from Exmouth which came with him, he had been in
great danger of his life and like to have been
murdered'.[4]

Raleigh, who was shortly to fall into the hands
of the rebels and imprisoned in the tower of St
Sidwell's church, saw to it that the story of his escape
was recounted to the Carews.

A second conference was held, at which it was
decided that the Carews should ride out to Clyst St
Mary to quell the rioters there. This time Sir Peter
dismounted as he approached the bridge, where the
guns were already loaded under the direction of John
Hammon, a blacksmith and an alien (probably a
Breton). Certainly Sir Peter would have been shot by
the gunner had not Hugh Osborne, a servant of
Serjeant Prideaux, held him back. The defenders,
nevertheless refused to speak with either of the
Carews, but agreed to parley with Sir Hugh Pollard,
whom they trusted, with Sir Thomas Denys, their
neighbour at Bicton, and a third gentleman, Thomas
Yarde; who were all thought to understand their
cause. They were to approach, however, without an
escort.

It was ten o'clock in the morning. The
discussion continued into the evening. The river there
was tidal. When one of Peter Carew's party tested the
depth of the water the gunners on the bridge believed

that he was looking for a ford to take them in the rear. The alarm was raised. The conference broke up and again nothing was achieved.

Back in Exeter at the Mermaid Inn the Carews held another conference. The envoys reported on their talks. The commons had undertaken to proceed no further provided that the Council made no alteration in religion, as it had been clearly stipulated in the will of King Henry: in other words they had stood by their original demands: it was no part of the duty of the justices to strike bargains with the rioters, their task had been to disarm and disperse them. Openly, sharply and in plain words the Carews inveighed against the two knights: it was Pollard who had failed to suppress the first demonstration at Sampford Courtenay and allowed it to spread through the countryside: he had now shown himself equally ineffective at Clyst St Mary. The two knights in their turn cast Sir Peter's own failure at Crediton against him. Charges and counter charges were made and in the increasing heat of the recriminations the meeting broke up and 'every man shifted for himself, some one way, some another'.[5]

News of these dissensions gave further encouragement to the rebels. More defensive works were raised and more highways blocked. The next morning the men who had taken part in the conference set out to return to their country seats. Many were taken prisoner on their way, several who escaped 'were driven to hide themselves in woods and in secret places in great peril and fear';[6] still others like Walter Raleigh were kept in durance during the whole time of the rebellion. Although Hooker states that they lived in hardship and under the daily threat of death there is no evidence that the commons intended in any way to injure them.

Very early that morning, however, Peter Carew, who had slept in the Mermaid, found an unblocked road and galloped post-haste eastward to report on the state of affairs to the Council. Although he had failed completely in his mission of pacification he had at least alerted John Blackaller, the Mayor of Exeter, to put the city in a state of defence: he had already agreed with the city councillors not to hold the long established midsummer eve celebration, in which the city officers, in company with representatives of the guilds, all in livery, carrying their cressets, banners and emblems, went in procession round the walls in a ritual inspection of its defences, and then sat down to a generous banquet. After the burning of the barns it was rightly feared that any small incident in which rebel sympathisers were involved might spark off a riot in the city. Instead, ten householders were appointed to do the round of the walls and, as a further precaution, it was ruled that the 'corporation of tailors, weavers and tuckers, and shoemakers, bakers and brewers shall ... bring for the watch ... ten men in harness, householders or discreet inhabitants'.[7]

In was then that Arundell made a miscalculation that was to prove fatal to the cause of the rebels. The capture of the Mount, followed by the fall of Plymouth, had encouraged him to expect Exeter to go the same way, if not at once, then after a short siege. Had he masked the city and marched to London as the Cornishmen had done in 1497, there was little more than local levies under the command of Lord Russell between him and the capital, and there was every chance that large numbers of sympathisers would join him on the way.

When Somerset declined Paget's proposal to put himself at the head of an army to suppress the rebellion, he had instead appointed Lord Russell, the Privy Seal. One of the sixteen Councillors named by Henry VIII to govern the country during Edward VI's minority, Russell had risen rapidly after joining the court in 1507 as a gentleman of the Privy Chamber. As a Dorsetshire squire he had attended Henry VIII at the capture of Tournai. Knighted in 1522, he was created Lord Russell in 1538, then appointed with almost regal powers President of the Council of the West, with jurisdiction over Devon, Cornwall, Dorset and Somerset: at its institution the Council was explicitly instructed to 'give straight charge and commandment to the people to conform themselves' to the new laws concerning religion. Made Lord High Admiral in 1540 Russell became Lord Privy Seal two years later.

Just four years before the rebellion he had commanded the musters of Devon in the French war and had successfully led the attack on the fortress of Boulogne. He was now in his fifty-sixth year. He was a dedicated and stern soldier, merciless to his enemies and with a reputation for brutality. As President of the Council of the West, a beneficiary of the spoils of monastic lands in Devon, and as an experienced commander he was a clear choice of the Council to restore the King's peace in the west. As Lord Admiral he had the additional task of protecting the south coast against threatened French landings.

On 25 June Russell duly was given authority to call upon all subjects to serve the King in the counties over which he had jurisdiction. Somerset, however, was still far from appreciating the seriousness of the rising: this is clear from the instructions he despatched to Russell: in places where he found people 'out of frame' he was to 'discover the cause thereof and travail by gentle persuasion to bring the people with gentleness to become obedient subjects': if foreign invasion threatened he was to set up beacons in accustomed places along the coast and take charge of the defence; clothiers, dyers, weavers, fullers and all other artificers were to be kept occupied so that they should have no leisure for unlawful assemblies, and all persons starting or spreading false rumours and alarms were to be committed to ward and punished. And above all he was to see that his Majesty's orders touching religion were well obeyed and executed'.[8] To assist him in this last task two divines, Dr Gregory and Dr Reynolds, were to accompany him. As chaplains to his army they were to bring the people back to their obedience 'by frequent and discreet preaching' in whatever place Russell should choose.[9]

Leaving London Russell joined his levies at Salisbury and made his way to Hinton St George, the seat of the Paulet family, which he made his temporary headquarters. It was there that Sir Peter Carew, who had left Exeter on 24 June, turning aside from the London road, reported on the events of the last few days around Exeter. Sir Peter advised Russell to proceed to Honiton, where the Carew mansion at Mohun's Ottery would give him a convenient base for action against the rebels. Russell on his side urged Carew to impress on the Council his need for further troops.

On reaching London Sir Peter, to his surprise, was reprimanded by Somerset for rousing the passions of the commons still further by burning down the barns: he had been sent, he was reminded, on a conciliatory mission. Carew, however, read out his instructions which authorised him to see that the laws were severely enforced, claiming that he had in no way exceeded his warrant. The Chancellor, Lord Rich, was unconvinced: Carew had required the King's commission under the Broad Seal for his actions. There was a charged debate in the Council. The government, anxious that it should not appear divided at such a moment of crisis, allowed the matter to go no further. Carew was formally exonerated and sent to join Lord Russell, taking with him letters promising him more men and money.

In London, however, all was not quiet. Earlier in the year there had been indications that the capital was in sympathy with the rebel cause, and it was now feared that it might open its gates to the rebels. As part of the attempt to enforce the changes in religion sermons had been preached against the old faith. Feelings ran high. When, in Lent, Hugh Latimer, now Russell's personal chaplain at Honiton, had preached at St Margaret's, Westminster, using foul and violent language against the old established religion, a riot followed. Latimer and other preachers were accused of fomenting rebellion. A note in the churchwarden's accounts giving the cost of 'mending the pews that were broken when Dr Latimer did preach' registers the event.[10] The government was further disturbed by recurring rumours that the Princess Mary was in league with the rebels, that she had sanctioned the rising and that her chaplains were among the insurgents. Somerset complained that 'her proceedings in matters of religion being well known had given no small encouragement to the rebels'. When offered the Prayer Book Mary proudly retorted: 'although the Council had forgotten the King her father and their oaths to observe his will, yet for herself she would observe his laws as he left them' until her brother was of years of discretion. Her father's will, she pointed out, had designedly been drawn up to restrain the Council from altering the religion of the country, therefore she refused to acknowledge the authority the Government had assumed in 'making (as they call it) laws both clean contrary to his proceedings and will and also against the custom of all Christendom and (in my conscience) against the law of God and his church'. And she added that if the realm was in disorder it was no fault of hers. Somerset, however, in her brother the King's name gave her licence 'to use her own services at her pleasure'.[11]

6. THE INVESTMENT OF EXETER

Lord Russell in the meantime remained increasingly anxious at his base at Honiton. The Council's orders sent secretly to the justices and gentry to arm their servants and tenants to serve under him had been largely ignored. He had only a small core of professional soldiers on whom he could rely, totally inadequate to meet the growing strength of the rebels who were now joined by a number of Devonshire gentlemen, including the Coffins of Portledge, who were later to become recusants.

Before moving to besiege Exeter, the men from Devon united with the Cornishmen in sending a joint manifesto to the Council in the form of fresh Articles, signed by the four 'chief captains' and the 'four governors of the camps': the governors were two priests, Roger Barett and John Thomson, and the Mayors of Bodmin and Torrington. Entitled the 'Articles of us commoners of Devon and Cornwall in divers camps east and west of Exeter', they were more detailed and explicit than the Articles sent from Bodmin. These Articles exist in several versions, with slight or negligible differences in phrasing, but substantially the same. One version only has a sixteenth Article demanding the surrender of hostages as a surety for their fulfilment: it runs: 'For the performance of these articles we will have four lords, eight knights, twelve esquires, and twenty yeomen pledges unto us until the King's Majesty have granted all these by Parliament'.

All the demands concern religion: there is no mention of the sheep tax, a grievance felt more in Devonshire than elsewhere, because it was largely a pastoral county with no acute enclosure problem. The tone of the document is peremptory, indicating the growing confidence of the rebels.

The first Article reads: 'We will have the general counsalls and the holy decrees of our forefathers observed, kept and performed, and whosoever shall gainsay them, we hold them as heretics'. Then in the second Article they again called for the enforcement of the will of Henry VIII. Touching the Eucharist and the reservation of the Sacrament the rebels were more emphatic, insisting that 'they which will not thereto consent we will have them die like heretics against the holy Catholic faith'. The earlier demands regarding baptism and the age-long customs were repeated: palms, ashes and other practices were to be restored and statues set up again in churches; 'we will not receive the new service', they protested, 'because it is but a Christmas game, but we will have our old service of Matins, Mass, Evensong and processions in Latin as it was before'; and they now added that priests in their sermons should ask prayers for the dead, who should also be remembered at Mass.

The commons had not forgotten Fr Moreman and Fr Crispyn who had been imprisoned in the Tower after the disturbances following the murder of Body: they asked that they should be released and given certain livings so that they could 'preach among us our Catholic faith'. And it was clearly an indication of their growing confidence that they demanded that Reginald Pole, then living abroad, should be sent for and promoted to the Council: Pole was the King's cousin, the son of Margaret Plantagenet, the daughter of Edward IV's brother, the

Duke of Clarence: he had denied the King's Supremacy over the Church and had refused to return to England on the condition laid down by Somerset, namely, that he should conform to the reformed religion. This demand for Pole's reinstatement implied a return to communion with Rome.

The final two demands were of a different kind. The first called for a restriction on the number of gentlemen's servants according to the amount of land they held, a request, it seems, to prevent their armed retainers imposing their will on the commons, particularly in enclosing land. The second required that half the abbey and chantry lands in every man's possession should be given back in order to establish two places in every county where devout persons could pray for the King and commonwealth, a proposal which would have saved from ruin the abbeys of Bodmin and Launceston in Cornwall, Plympton and Tavistock in Devon and Glastonbury and Cleeve in Somerset.

The Articles concluded with a petition that Humphry Arundell and Henry Bray, the Mayor of Bodmin, should be given a safe conduct in order to explain their grievances to the King.

Intent now on capturing Exeter, Arundell sent messengers to the Mayor, John Blackaller, calling on him to join the Rising: the resources of the city in arms, money and recruits would add greatly to his strength. His approach, however, was rejected. But all the time the rebel camp was growing. John Hooker, unquestionably prejudiced against the rebels, was then in Exeter and noted that 'many of them brought their wives, horses and panniers, persuading themselves and promising them by such a day and upon such an hour to enter into the city, and then to measure velvets and silks by the bow and to load their horses with plate and money and other great riches'.[1]

That this was the intention of the rebels is unlikely. The Mayor, however, answered the rebels with a 'full, resolute and direct answer that they would not join or deal with them at all'. At this Arundell sent further messages, now warning Blackaller that he would besiege the city if his demand that they should maintain the old Catholic faith was rejected. The answer again was a plain refusal.[2]

No doubt Arundell was relying on the known attachment of the citizens to the old religion for a favourable response. Unlike other large cities, such as London and Bristol that were open to the commerce of the world, Exeter had remained staunchly conservative and opposed, as a contemporary expressed it, to 'the fashion of the world as goeth now': the city traded very little with Holland and Germany, through which the teachings of the Continental reformers entered the country. Only recently it had given evidence of its opposition to religious reforms. Thomas Dusgate, for example, a Fellow of Corpus Christi, Cambridge, a priest who had visited Luther, had married and returned to Exeter, where he had affixed bills on the door of the cathedral denouncing the Pope as anti-Christ. After confessing his action before the city magistrates he had been handed over to the ecclesiastical authorities, condemned as a heretic and on 5 January 1531 burned at the stake just two miles outside the city walls: a brief account of his life, which remains in manuscript, was compiled by Ralph Morice, Cranmer's secretary. Again, four years later, when St Nicholas's Priory, along with the smaller monastic houses, was suppressed and two Breton carvers were busy dismantling the rood screen, women reputed to be men in disguise broke into the church and scared them off.

As a body the cathedral clergy were every bit as opposed to religious reform as the rebels. John Veysey, the bishop of Exeter since 1517, had been appointed by Henry VIII tutor to Princess Mary and was known for his sympathy with the cause of Queen Catherine. Although his duties at court occupied a great deal of his time he administered his diocese with vigour: incumbents were made to reside in their living and the clergy to give instruction to their people, to Cornishmen, in Cornish, every Sunday. Until compelled by his conscience to live abroad Reginald Pole had been Dean of the cathedral since 1527. When his successor, Simon Heynes, was commissioned by the King in 1535 'to preach against the supremacy of the Pope and reconcile the minds of students to its abolition' he came up against determined opposition from the chapter, who, in 1543, had him imprisoned on the charge of alienating cathedral property. Although there was no question about the canons' devotion to what Hooker calls 'Popish superstitions', yet when the city came to be besieged they stood by the civic authorities. Heynes, with his preaching zeal, had already converted a number of leading citizens to the Protestant faith. 'Marvellously hated and maligned,' as Hooker writes, he had the cathedral clergy in thrall. Fr Crispyn, who might have swayed the canons in favour of the rebels, was now in the Tower of London for preaching at Marldon against the Protestant doctrine of Scripture.

Among the citizens, nevertheless, there was a small, very active, anti-papal body. There were two parties, confesses Hooker himself, 'the one and the greater number were of the old stamp and of the Romish religion, the other being of the lesser number were of a contrary mind and disposition'. The former, continues Hooker, 'were so addicted to their own fantasies ... that they cannot abide or hear of any other religion than that they were first noselled in'.(3)

Nevertheless, Blackaller, 'who had no love for religious changes ... had less for treason and insurrection', finally replied to the rebels that if they wanted to take Exeter they would have to force their way into the city.

Blackaller then ordered the five great gates of the city to be closed, but not before a large number of sympathisers had left to join the rebels. This, however, proved damaging to their cause: had they remained inside the walls there would have been more chance of a successful uprising against the Mayor; they would also have added to the demand on the very limited supply of food and very probably have brought the city to surrender before the siege could be rased by the government troops.

Finally, on 2 July, in a last attempt to take possession of the city peacefully, the massed commons, now numbering many thousands, processed across the river past the church of St Thomas towards the West Gate in the same manner in which they had marched across Bodmin moor. Behind the banner of the Five Wounds walked the priests in their chasubles, following the canopy under which was carried the Blessed Sacrament. Behind them came the people chanting the familiar

Edward VI

Reliquary of St Petroc. Bodmin Priory

Sampford Courtenay: Courthouse and Church

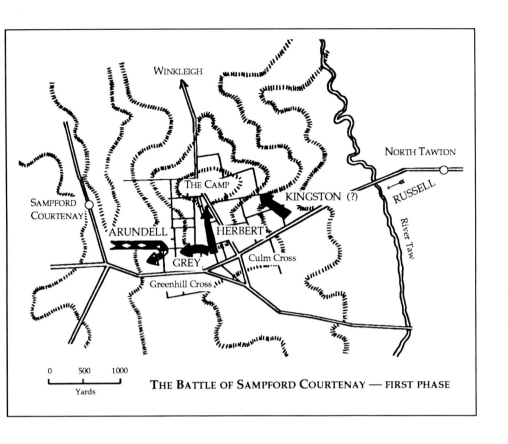

WINKLEIGH

NORTH TAWTON

THE CAMP

KINGSTON (?)

RUSSELL

SAMPFORD
COURTENAY

River Taw

ARUNDELL

HERBERT

GREY

Culm Cross

Greenhill Cross

| 0 | 500 | 1000 |

Yards

THE BATTLE OF SAMPFORD COURTENAY — FIRST PHASE

The old approach to Crediton, scene of the burning barns

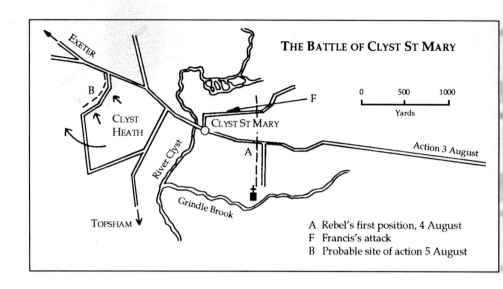

THE BATTLE OF CLYST ST MARY

EXETER

B

CLYST HEATH

CLYST ST MARY

F

River Clyst

A

Grindle Brook

TOPSHAM

0   500   1000
Yards

Action 3 August

A Rebel's first position, 4 August
F Francis's attack
B Probable site of action 5 August

Battlefield of Fenny Bridges

Lord Russell

Sir Peter Carew

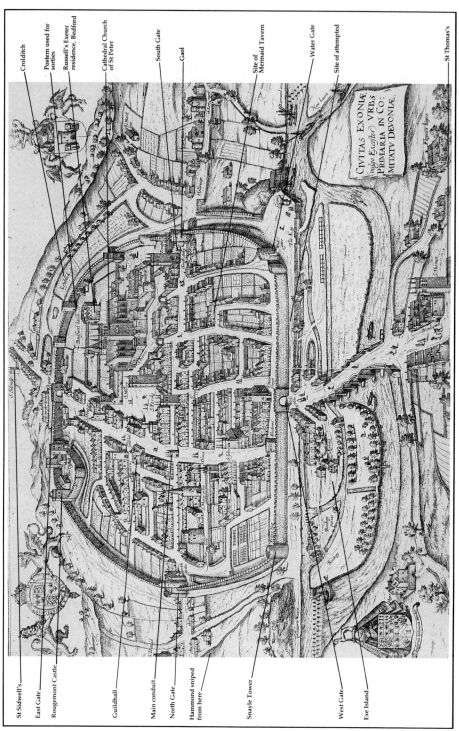

Hooker's map of Exeter

St Sidwell's

East Gate

Rougemont Castle

Guildhall

Main conduit

North Gate

Hammond sniped from here

Snayle Tower

West Gate

Exe Island

Crolditch

Postern used for sorties

Russell's Exeter residence, Bedford

Cathedral Church of St Peter

South Gate

Gaol

Site of Mermaid Tavern

Water Gate

Site of attempted

St Thomas's

CIVITAS EXONIÆ
(vulgo Excester) VRB.s
PRIMARIA IN CO:
MITATV DEVONIÆ.

Pages from the manuscript of Hooker's history of Exeter

The banner of the Five Wounds

Eucharistic hymns. As they halted at the West Gate a herald came forward and called upon the inhabitants to surrender the city without a fight and join their fellow countrymen in their demand that the late King's will should be honoured.

Blackaller himself shouted a defiant answer and then set about making last arrangements to withstand a siege. With the civic officers he 'provided all things meet and necessary to defend themselves and annoy the enemy'. The city was searched for armour, men were mustered, soldiers retained, captains appointed in every ward, wardens assigned for the day and watchmen for the night, ordnance placed at the gates and on the walls, mounts erected in convenient places and at the foot of St Edmund's bridge a barrier raised, into which were fixed scores of sharp spikes; in fact everything was made ready against a siege.

On the same day the rebels encircled the city from St David's Down to St Sidwell's church across the wide waste of the Southernhay, even to the South Gate along the open banks and flats by the river from the Water Gate past West Gate to Snayle Tower. They numbered several thousand in all. Guards were posted, so that no one could pass into or out of the city and no victuals carried in. Then 'having penned in and shut up the townsmen in a coup or mew', they placed their ordnance at every gate and at points against the walls, then set about breaking up the pipes and conduits, not only to cut off the city's water supply, but also to make lead pellets and shot for their weapons. The city, however, set though it was on a steep hill, was well provided with springs and was to suffer no shortage of water.

It was probably on the day the siege began that Russell reached Honiton, just sixteen miles from the city: he had advanced slowly from Hinton St George in Somerset along the main artery west: it was a busy town with numerous inns, a convenient stopping place for travellers before continuing on their journey east through the hills; and just five miles to the north in the Blackdown Hills was the former Cistercian monastery of Dunkeswell, founded in 1211, but now in the possession of Lord Russell himself. As the numbers of the rebels increased he dithered nervously at his base: his force probably numbered little more than a hundred: many of the men who had at first offered to serve under him had fallen away. There could be no question of his advancing to Exeter. Hooker summarised his situation: 'having a very small guard about him, he lived in more fear than he was feared, for the rebels daily increased and his company decreased and shrank away and he was not altogether assured of them which remained'.[4] It would seem that the majority of the gentry were now waiting to see which side won before committing themselves, while the noblemen were unwilling to serve under the command of a man whom they regarded as an upstart.

Russell had been in Honiton about a week when on 9 July reports reached him that Exeter had food for only two days and that the city was expected to fall any hour. At the same time there were rumours of disturbances in Salisbury. Russell vacillated. Fearing to be cut off in his rear he decided to retreat to Sherborne, where the castle would bar the advance of the insurgents and to wait there for the arrival of reinforcements. 'And as soon as he was departed from Honiton,' writes Hooker, 'Sir Peter Carew, having knowledge thereof, took his horse at Mohun's Ottery and rode up to the Black Down and there met with him; and then having some speeches and conferences with him' Carew convinced him that a withdrawal would only encourage the enemy, bring about the 'undoing of the whole country' and do great dishonour to himself 'if he should now ... give the enemy scope and liberty to go forward'. Russell allowed himself to be persuaded and returned to Honiton. 'And true it was,' concludes Hooker,' that if he had departed according to his first determination, there had grown thereby a greater fire than all the waters in five shires about would have been able to have quenched'.(5)

Russell had no alternative but to remain at Honiton watching to see what course the siege would take until reinforcements reached him.

7. LORD RUSSELL AT HONITON

If Russell had no reason to fear disturbances in the rear of his position at Honiton, there was growing unrest in other parts of the country. There were stirrings of rebellion in Yorkshire, Norfolk, Suffolk and, worst of all, in Oxfordshire where, as in Devon and Cornwall, the defiance was religious in character. The Treasury was empty. While the Protector was unwilling to take more than half measures the Council acted. The Protestant Lords, anxious to retain their gains from the despoliation of the monasteries, raised money by every possible shift. Before the western rebellion was finally crushed Warwick, Herbert, Southampton, Dorset, Paget, Russell himself, Sir Thomas Wentworth, Huntingdon, Cobham and others subscribed among themselves a hundred thousand pounds.[1] The Marquis of Northampton, the brother of Catherine Parr, set off with fifteen hundred men to Norfolk; Lord Grey de Wilton went west with the Lanzknechts, the German mercenaries that had been held in readiness for the Scottish campaign, together with three hundred Italian musketeers and some artillery, altogether more than a thousand men: he was to deal with the troubles in Oxfordshire and Buckinghamshire, then go on to join Russell at Honiton; Sir William Herbert set out for Wales to raise the force of the Borders and march them across the Somerset flats towards the South West.

Herbert was a soldier adventurer whose career had followed a pattern not unlike that of Peter Carew. Aubrey, the biographer, speaks of him as 'a mad, young fighting fellow': he had served in the French army on fleeing England after killing a mercer from Bristol. In 1542, and again two years later, he and his wife Anne, the younger sister of Henry VIII's Queen, Catherine Parr, received the estates of Wilton Abbey where he had destroyed the monastic buildings to erect his splendid mansion: when his park there had been invaded by protesters he had dealt brutally with them. In 1546 he was appointed steward of much of the royal estates in the West and in the same year was made an executor of Henry's will; in the year of the rebellion he was further advanced to become Master of Horse. By the time he set out to join Russell he had raised a force of two thousand from his Welsh estates.

Lord Grey, the second commander sent to suppress the Western Rising, had served under Russell in the expedition to France in 1544: as Lieutenant of Boulogne in 1546 he had destroyed the fortress of Chatillon, razing it to the ground. In the first year of Edward's reign Grey, then a Field Marshal, was sent to Scotland where, in the battle of Pinkie Cleugh on 10 September, he received a great wound in his mouth with a pike which struck him through his tongue and penetrated three fingers deep into the roof of his mouth. Both he and Herbert were experienced, ruthless and formidable commanders.

When news of the investment of Exeter reached London there was alarm in the city. Fearing that the rebels would soon resume their march, the Council gave orders for the destruction of the bridge over the Thames at Staines. On 18 July a state of martial law was proclaimed. Two days later picked livery men from each company were instructed to keep watch at every gate from five in the morning until eight at night when the gates were closed; orders were given for the authorities to have ready their 'harness, guns, bows and other weapons' against an assault; large pieces of the King's brass ordnance were brought from the Tower and mounted on the city gates and in places on the walls.

At the height of the panic the Council wrote again to Princess Mary in the hope of persuading her to forgo her licence for the celebration of Mass in her house at Kenninghall, complaining that she was encouraging the rebels by her 'persistence in the use of the old Mass'; in addition they accused certain servants of hers of being active agents of the rebels. On 20 July she replied that 'as for Devonshire no indifferent person can lay their doings to my charge' and went on to blame the disturbances on the Council's 'new alterations and unlawful liberties' rather than on 'my doings who am (God take me to witness) inquieted therewith'.[2]

These frantic preparations for the defence of the city were reported to the Emperor Charles V by his ambassador in London. More mercenaries, he wrote, had been sent for from Boulogne, and this had aroused the wrath of the citizens who had threatened not to leave a foreigner alive in London: all mercenaries were considered brutal: in 1516 the Venetian ambassador had written to the Doge that 'they do not content themselves with plundering, but burn and kill, filling every place with death and slaughter'. While every nation in Europe used mercenaries, mainly German, Swiss, Italian or Dutch, in their Continental wars, none had yet employed them in their domestic conflicts: it was an innovation that brought odium on the Council and indicated the extent of its nervous alarm: mercenaries had provided the core of the government forces on the Borders, perhaps five thousand in all; others were now on their way north or awaiting transport at Boulogne. Somerset had to nurse these resources in foreign troops, for disaffection was so widespread in the southern counties that little reliance could be placed on local levies: recruitment abroad, moreover, was difficult: men were reluctant to sign on for service in England because pay was poor and there were tales of the hostility of Englishmen to foreigners; they were also unwilling to become embroiled in civil war. Nevertheless, on 10 July Somerset, appreciating at last Russell's need for help, agreed to release a few of his valuable mercenaries, a hundred and fifty Italian arquebusiers, to stiffen his troops.

At the same time as Somerset detailed mercenaries to march west he pointed out to Russell that while waiting for more troops he could employ himself cutting off sources of food supples from the besieging rebel army and prevent it from gathering recruits: as a means of doing this he suggested that he should spread reports of their atrocities, no matter whether true or false, in the countryside: Hooker only was impressed and without evidence wrote that Arundell's forces increased through intimidation, whereas in fact hardly anyone could be found to support Russell, who was now told that he should note the names of those refusing to join him, so that they could be duly dealt with after the rebellion was over. Russell, never afraid to resort to systematic terrorism could do little apart from executing a spy who was caught carrying a circular from the rebel leaders to be read from the pulpits of neighbouring counties.

All through the month of July Cranmer was busy in London seeking to enforce vigorously the religious changes. Sermons were drafted for all curates to read in their churches 'to preserve the people in their obedience and to set out the evil and mischief of the present disturbances'.[3] On the day appointed for the sermon to be read a fast was to be observed and 'the people exhorted ... to put aside delicious and superfluous feeding and sumptuous apparel ... and to call on Almighty God for mercy and grace'.[4] On 21 July, while Russell was still waiting nervously at Honiton, Cranmer himself preached at St Paul's before the Mayor and most of the aldermen: it was noticed that he had abandoned vestments, mitre and cross and had on a satin cap throughout the service: the congregation was told that the commotions in the west and elsewhere were a plague brought on by the devil who was at work among the common sort of people: this indeed might have been expected of Cranmer who, like Luther, had no time for peasants and common folk. The service ended with a long prayer composed by the Archbishop for the occasion in which the congregation confessed to the Lord that they had 'deserved this rod' with which they had been chastised.[5]

After the service the Archbishop's chaplain preached on the same theme to a larger crowd in St Paul's churchyard. The next day gallows were set up in Aldgate, where a tailor, arrested at Rainsford in Essex on suspicion of being a rebel, was executed; and also in Southwark, where a man from Boulogne suffered the same fate for acting in a manner that was thought suspicious.

Russell remained at Honiton, unable to advance. Owing to what Hooker calls the 'evil inclination of the people' he had little success in raising levies from Somerset. The Council meanwhile could do little more than send him unwanted advice and a series of proclamations. Possibly Somerset considered Russell too old at the age of sixty-three to take vigorous action against the rebels. He advised him while waiting to march on Exeter to infiltrate spies into the enemy encampment and to start at once to deprive their forces of supplies by stripping the whole area surrounding their encampments of victuals. Then on 22 July he proposed that when Russell received the eight hundred foreign footmen he could 'put them on horseback, getting horses from the countryside': this, he said, would give him the great advantage of mounted troops, enable him to choose a favourable point for engaging the enemy, whom he would thus be able to overcome though they might be ten times more numerous.[6] Russell replied angrily. He regarded Somerset's advice on tactics an insult to a seasoned commander: he had been sent horsemen when he required regular footmen; he was convinced that cavalry were unsuited to operate in the narrow lanes between the deep hedges of the Devonshire countryside. He needed ammunition, men and money, not advice; when he pointed out that the men of Somerset were reluctant to join him he was told 'to hang two or three of them and cause them to be executed as traitors'; and as for ammunition he could easily manufacture his own: 'as to shot,' he was told, 'shift is to be made to buy lead whereof we doubt not there is plenty within the limits of your commission'.[7]

The proclamations sent to Russell for publication in the absence of troops threatened all rebels who did not submit with instant forfeiture of their lands and copyholds, a measure which the Council hoped 'shall be as much a terror as any other thing that can possibly be devised'.[8] The Council also proposed extending the threat of forfeiture to all who spread abroad Arundell's propaganda or supplied his forces with victuals. About the same time Russell was alerted to the intention of the French 'at this present time to land in Cornwall or Devonshire and there, as our espyall showeth, to take a gentleman's house which is almost an isle and more than half environed in the sea'. This was a reference to Mount St Michael, which had been in the hands of the rebels since the first weeks of the Rising.

While Grey was making for Oxfordshire, Herbert mustering his forces in Wales, and the Earl of Warwick, whose help Russell had requested, was prevented from marching west by troubles in the home counties, Russell saw to it that such forces as he had were awarded their pay. With the help of three leading merchants of Exeter, Thomas Prestwood, a former Mayor, John Bodley and John Peryam, men of great wealth, whose interest it was to save the city from destruction, he managed to obtain on their credit from the merchants of Bristol, Lynn, Taunton and elsewhere 'such a mass of money which when he had received his grief was eased'.[9] This enabled him to replenish his supplies and raise a number of men. Nevertheless he continued to complain. The Council could only remind him, as it had done earlier, that the Treasury was empty and suggested that there were doubtless church goods which he could seize 'as belike the rebels do', a baseless charge against the rebels, but a suggestion which Russell was quick to act on. The townspeople of Ashburton contributed two chalices and a pyx for ten pounds 'with which money they served the King's majesty against the rebels'. At Tavistock, where Russell enjoyed the spoils of the religious house, the loyalists sold sufficient plate and vestments to enable Russell to enlist another twenty men.

While waiting still at Honiton for the arrival of reinforcements Russell would have received for distribution the first of the Council's replies to the Articles drawn up jointly by the rebels at Crediton. It carried the King's signature and was addressed to his people assembled in Devonshire. Drawn up by Somerset the reply is in part conciliatory, in part contemptuous in tone. It seeks to answer each article, though not in order. 'As for Mass,' it states, 'the learned clergy have brought this to the very use as Christ left it, as the apostles used it and as the holy fathers delivered it, indeed somewhat altered from that the Popes of Rome for their lucre brought it'.[10] Towards the close the reply employs overt threats: 'we have condescended out of love,' it runs, 'to write rather than war against you as rebels, but unless you repent we will extend our princely power and draw the sword against you as against infidels and Turks'.

Somerset was still in favour of leniency but was not prepared to make any concession in matters of religion, which was for him an affair of state and as such exclusively within the prerogative of Parliament. This meant that he was now faced not with riots or disturbances as in other parts of the country, but with open rebellion.

A second reply followed, dated 24 July. It refers to the earlier answer and is addressed to the four captains and four governors of the camps. It covers the same ground as the first. Still hoping to convert the rebels to the religious reforms, yet a third answer was despatched before the end of the month. It was the work of a Cornishman, Nicholas Udall, a classical scholar, a distinguished headmaster of Eton, and a prolific pamphleteer. He wrote as a westcountryman addressing his 'simple and plain speaking Cornishmen' who had been aroused by the 'sinister persuasion of certain seditious papists, whelps of the Roman litter, abusing your simplicity and lightness of credit'. This document is a compendium of Protestant doctrine in its first draft which in its essentials was to survive the Marian restoration of Catholicism: just as the stiff-necked and ungrateful Jews, it began, had rebelled against God who had delivered them from Egypt, so the rebels have turned against the government which had delivered them from the slavery of superstition and Popery. As for palms and ashes, 'how few of you simple and unlettered folk,' writes Udall, 'can tell what ... (they) mean, wherefor they were given and what they signify'. Henry VIII's Articles, which they clamoured for, had been the work of certain Papists: being violently wrong, they had been rightly repealed by Parliament. Touching the difficulty the Cornishmen had in understanding English Udall suggested that the new service might in time be turned into Cornish, a proposal which, if it had been carried out, would have meant that the Prayer Book might never have become the chief means of spreading the English language in the Duchy.[11]

Udall, however, went so far as to draft a petition for a Cornish Prayer Book to be submitted by the rebels for the King's approval, adding that 'if you had (I say) made such an humble and godly request as this I doubt not but the King ... would have provided for the accomplishment of your desires'.[12]

From Article to Article Udall shifted in his reply from threat, to enticement and finally to pleading 'to Devonshire men and Cornish men, both captains and campers, to quit the 'few malicious papist agitators' and return to the King's obedience.

8. EXETER UNDER SIEGE

With the majority of citizens of Exeter, especially in the South Gate area, and others outside the walls in Southernhay, in sympathy with the rebel cause, Arundell did not expect to have to mount a protracted siege when on 2 July he began the encirclement of the city. Hooker, who was then in Exeter, reckoned that the besieging force at first numbered no more than two thousand, but according to another chronicler, Holinshed, it swelled to some ten thousand in the course of the month: this may well be an exaggeration, for the city itself, ranking fifth or sixth among the provincial cities, was estimated to have a population of about eight thousand.

The rebel army, however, was not equipped to undertake the siege of a large city. It had no siege train that could make a breach in the walls: what guns it possessed were of small calibre taken from the seaports and mounted on trucks: incapable of making an impression on the city's defences, they could only be positioned on high ground outside the North Gate from which they could fire over the walls into the main streets.

But in the rebel ranks were a number of Cornish tinners experienced in sapping and mining. Filling with gunpowder and pitch a gallery which they drove under the West Gate, they planned to detonate it in the darkness of the night while a storming party stood by to burst through the breach. But the plan miscarried. Within the walls there happened to be a Teignmouth man, John Newcombe, also a miner, who heard the digging and at once warned an alderman friend, William Hurst, of the danger. Borrowing a large flat pan filled with water Newcombe moved it here and there measuring the line and extent of the mining by the tremors on the water's surface. The Mayor was at once informed. No time was lost. Under Newcombe's directions a counter mine was dug. Then using the advantage of the steep slope of the hill towards the West Gate, Newcombe got all householders on the side of the gate where the miners were at work to place a tub filled with water outside their door. At a given signal the tubs were emptied and the water cascaded down the street into the shaft of the counter mine. The powder was rendered useless and the mine abandoned.

Another plan was formed, this time by a skilled gunner, a Breton, stationed on St David's hill outside the North Gate. He claimed that he could lay down a barrage of incendiary shot which would set fire to the city and destroy it within four hours. A day and time were fixed for the bombardment to begin. It was only the intervention of Robert Welsh, the vicar of St Thomas's, Exe Island, outside the West Gate, a Cornishman from Penryn, that stayed him. Hooker, who knew the man well, gives an attractive portrait of him. 'This man,' he writes, 'had many good things in him: he was of no great stature but well-set and compact; he was a very good wrestler, shot well both in the long bow and also in the cross bow; he handled his hand gun and piece very well; he was a very good woodsman ... a companion in any exercises or activity and of a courteous and gentle behaviour'.[1] Although very active among the rebels he was not prepared to see the city destroyed. Collecting a number of rebels he stayed the gunner. 'For (saith he) do what you can by policy, force or dint of sword to take the city, I will join with you and do my best, but to burn the city ... I will never consent thereto but will here stand with all my power against you'.[2]

Unable to break into the city Arundell's men now tried to wear down the citizens by constant harrying. At times they would approach the walls with scaling ladders as if they were going to attempt an assault. On one occasion they tried to burn down the South Gate by pushing against it a cart filled with straw and dry hay and setting it alight. To foil such tactics the defenders brought out some old 'great port pieces' used when the city was last besieged in 1497: these were guns with a muzzle of twelve inches, with barrels bound together with iron hoops and mounted on a stand of logs. Loaded with flint and metal they were brought to the South and West Gates, which were suddenly opened so that a murderous shower of shot could be discharged. These gates were then left permanently open and in their place earthen ramparts were erected, which formed barriers that were both stronger and more easily defended.

Intermittent sniping from the houses in the suburbs played a large part in wearing down the nerves of the defenders. Worst exposed to the shot were the houses in the street running down to the West Gate, which were not masked by the walls: 'some thereby were killed and many hurt'. In retaliation the defenders made sallies from the city in order to demolish the suburban houses from which the firing came. But the citizens had no means of countering the fire of 'their great ordnance' which they had positioned to fire into the centre of the city so that 'none could go but in peril and danger of their shot': the citizens could only protect themselves from these guns 'by making certain mounts to shadow the streets'. All the same, as Hooker admits, they practised 'divers other devices to the continual annoyance of the city ... but none so grievous and dangerous ... to be compared to the perils which were within the walls among themselves'.[3]

All through the siege messages were passed from time to time between the citizens and the rebels outside the walls. The 'favourers of the old Romish religion', as Hooker calls them, started parleying secretly with the besiegers; then they sent messages attached to arrowheads; and whenever a truce was arranged the citizens held meetings with the besiegers to discuss possible terms of surrender. Nothing came of the conferences. Each time the rebels demanded an exchange of hostages as a surety for the safety of those engaged in the talks. This, according to Hooker, who again reveals his prejudices, was an unequal bargain, for while the rebels demanded that some leading citizens should be handed over, they on their side would send only 'the refuse, the scum and the rascals of the whole country', though Hooker was forced to admit, these were their leaders: 'the worse the man,' he writes, 'the greater his authority among them, which was good enough for so wicked a matter'.

There was an occasion when the city might have fallen to the rebels: the Mayor had summoned the citizens to gather with their arms for a review at the Guildhall. The majority of the assembly made it clear that their sympathy lay with the rebels' cause. It was a dangerous situation for the defenders, and made worse when one of the papists, as Hooker calls them, Richard Taylor, a clothier, intending to cause a

riot and wrest control of the city from Blackaller, took
his bow and 'minding to have stricken the man to
whom he levelled the shot, he struck his own and best
friend, John Petre, the King's Customer (Custom
House Officer)', a brother of Sir William Petre, the
Secretary of State and probably a Catholic like the
majority of the crowd: this gentleman of good
countenance and credit, as Hooker describes John
Petre, would have died of his wound had not the
arrow struck him on one of his rib bones: in deep
distress at what he had done Taylor thought no more
of creating a riot: 'a great muttering was likely to
have bred a tumult but the matter being known it was
appeased'.(4) To avert further trouble a special
company numbering some hundred citizens was
formed to patrol the streets day and night in order to
guard against possible treachery. This precaution may
well have saved the city, for, a short time afterwards,
the soldiers in charge of the castle were suborned to
receive a party of rebels at the postern on a fixed day
and hour. But very shortly before the time a patrol
arrived to inspect the garrison and uncovered the plot.
'Whether the matter were mistrusted or whether it
pleased God to move the hearts of certain men' to
inspect the castle 'it is most certain ... the treachery
was espied and the practices discovered and their
whole devices prevented'.(5) At another time a
member of the city Council, John Walcott, on the
morning it was his turn to be captain of the watch,
thinking he could negotiate a peace, went with two
companions to the West Gate where he started talking
with the rebels. He then passed on through the wicket
gate carrying his keys: nothing was thought of this
since he was a respected civic officer. Crossing into

the rebel lines he spent some hours in conference with
their leaders. It is not known what offers, if any, were
made. But tempers became short and the Councillor
managed with difficulty to get back into the city, but
not without leaving his two companions as hostages.
He was severely reprimanded but no further action
was taken against him.

It was probably members of the special patrol
established after the Guildhall incident that formed
the nucleus of the parties organised to raid the enemy
lines. In one of the more successful sallies they
returned with a number of prisoners, a few small guns
and other spoil, but at the cost of several casualties:
John Symons, a cook, was killed and John Drake, a
former sheriff, returned with an arrow through both
cheeks.

These skirmishes, however, led to rivalries
between the two principal raiding parties, one led by
John Courtenay, a younger son of Sir William
Courtenay of Powderham and a soldier of experience,
and Bernard Duffield, a servant of Lord Russell and
keeper of his house near the wall just south of the East
Gate. Courtenay argued that sorties should not be
made except in furtherance of an overall defence plan,
while Duffield insisted that raids should continue as
before. Asked to adjudicate, the Mayor decided in
favour of Courtenay. In apoplectic fury Duffield
swore at the Mayor in 'such loud and disordered
speeches' that he had to be put in gaol. This was not
the end. Duffield's daughter demanded to see her
father and when she was refused she immediately
'waxed so warm that she not only used very unseemly
terms and speeches unto the Mayor but also, contrary
to the modesty and shamefacedness required in a

woman, especially young and unmarried, ran most violently upon him and struck him in the face'.[6] Soldiers had to be called upon to protect the lady from being drawn forcibly from her father's house. Blackaller's calm handling of the crisis again prevented a riot.

All this time Russell was unable to advance. Lord Grey, whose force was expected soon after the middle of July, had been delayed by disturbances in Oxfordshire and in neighbouring Buckinghamshire. In Oxfordshire, though not to the same extent in bordering counties, the grievances were religious in origin. The Italian Reformer, Pietro Martire Vermigli, better known as Peter Martyr, whose work on the Eucharist Udall was engaged in translating at the time he drew up his reply to the Articles of the rebels, had been propagating his teachings in Oxford: a former Augustinian canon, he had come to England at Cranmer's invitation, had assisted the Archbishop in his preparation of the Prayer Book and in the year of the rebellion had been appointed Regius Professor of Divinity in the university. His lectures on the Eucharist, in which he had rejected the doctrine of the Real Presence and the notion of sacrifice in the Mass, had caused a stir in the Colleges, which spilled over into the countryside. The whole of Oxfordshire was in turmoil. As in Cornwall it was an alliance of priests, yeomen and peasants, but unlike Cornwall, it had no organisation or leader. The assemblies of the people were quickly and brutally put down by Grey's mercenaries. It was the instigators who were the main sufferers. The rope was used to give force to the arguments of Peter Martyr. On 19 July, eager to hurry on to join Russell at Honiton, Grey summoned the sheriffs and gave them orders. To start with, a dozen leaders of the rebellion were to be executed, three to be hanged in Oxford, another three in Banbury, one each in Wallington, Islip, Deddington, Bicester, Chipping Norton and Bloxham, and two more selected by the justices at Thame. Four of the victims were priests who were hanged from the towers of their own churches. The bells which had been rung to arouse the peasants were taken down and sold for the benefit of the government, 'leaving one only of the smallest size'[7] to tinkle for the English Prayers, altogether a rehearsal on a smaller scale for what was soon to be witnessed in the South West. In London, Grey's action was highly commended. The Secretary of State, Sir Thomas Smith, wrote to the young William Cecil, Somerset's secretary, that the executions were worth ten thousand proclamations in this desperate state of the country.

At Oxford Peter Martyr continued as Regius Professor until the end of the reign but in the face of increasing opposition to his doctrines. 'You would hardly believe,' he wrote in April 1551 to his friend the Swiss Reformer, Henry Bullinger, 'with what bitterness, obstinacy, perverseness and inflexibility of mind we are resisted by our adversaries, and especially on this very subject (the Eucharist)'.[8]

9. FENNY BRIDGES AND WOODBURY COMMON

Throughout July Arundell was prevented from advancing by the continuing resistance of Exeter, while Russell remained immobilised at Honiton for lack of reinforcements: the Carews had joined him with a contingent raised from Dorset, but hardly large enough to make good Russell's losses through desertion.

It was only with the arrival of one hundred and fifty Italian arquebusiers under the command of the Genoese nobleman, Paolo Batista Spinola, around the 21 July that Russell felt strong enough to make a reconnaissance in force while awaiting the arrival of Grey's troops from Oxfordshire and Herbert's from the Borders. With a strong well-equipped patrol he set out in the direction of Exeter, but finding his way blocked made a diversion south to Ottery St Mary, a town about nine miles from Exeter on a small hill with the ground falling away on every side except to the east. After spending a nervous night there he planned to ride over West Hill to view from a distance the situation round Exeter. But again he came up against road-blocks and in a fit of frustration burned down Ottery St Mary and all the houses on the road back to Honiton.

In the course of reconnaissance Russell had encountered a section of Arundell's army. In the skirmish that followed Russell got the better of the rebels thanks to the Italian arquebusiers, though his archers proved no match for the rebel bowmen: their shafts went wide, were retrieved by the rebels and shot back.

The gap between the forces was narrow: though Russell had a core of professional soldiers, the Cornishmen were highly respected for their courage and their skill as archers: in this and later encounters it was largely a battle between the arquebus and the long bow. Robert Smyth, the rebel leader, favoured the bow's simplicity, its longer range and the rapid rate at which its arrows could be discharged, while men had to be trained to fire the arquebus and recharge it efficiently: the series of battles that followed in the last days of the western rebellion did nothing to settle the controversy on the comparative value of the two weapons, which continued for the next fifty years.

Arundell now was anxious to get his blow in before Russell received further reinforcements, for Grey was only a few days march from Honiton and Herbert a short distance behind him. This decision, however, may well have proved an error, for it forced Russell into action, whereas had he delayed another two or three days in Honiton, Exeter would probably have fallen. In the last week of July, therefore, Arundell, leaving a containing force round Exeter, advanced as far as Fenny Bridges over the river Otter about two miles from Honiton: here the river divided into four branches with arms driving tucking mills to wash woollen cloths and to work other mills for grinding corn. On the advice of the Carews, Russell decided to attack. The rebels had fortified one end of the bridges and then, with banners flying, had deployed their main force in the field below where they hoped to cut off Russell's retreat to Honiton.

Russell, underestimating the determination of the enemy, attempted to take the bridges by storm, but 'after trying all policies he could devise' without incurring undue losses he fell back. After re-forming his troops, he sent in a strong detachment of arquebusiers and at the same time swept the far end of the bridges with cannon fire. He succeeded in clearing the bridges of the defenders, but at the cost of several casualties, including Sir Gawen Carew, who was wounded in the arm by an arrow. Russell's main body then crossed the bridges and charged the rebels in the field below. After a fierce encounter 'not without good store of blow and bloodshed' Russell got the upper hand. The rebels broke and fled. Thinking their victory complete, Russell's 'soldiers and serving men gave them all to the spoil' only to be surprised by a contingent of a hundred or more Cornishmen under Robert Smyth of St Germans, who 'taking these spoilers napping, (made them) pay dearly for their wares'. Establishing some sort of battle line Russell 'gave onset upon them, between whom the fight for a time was very sharp and cruel. For the Cornishmen were very lusty and fresh and full bent to fight out the matter: nevertheless in the end they were overthrown and their captain whose comb was cut, showed a fair pair of heels and fled away. In these two fights there were reported to be slain about three hundred rebels which were very tall men, lusty and of great courage and who in a good cause might have done better service'.[1] It was said that Russell lost three hundred men that day. It is not known for certain how many rebels fell.

Russell's men pursued the rebels for close on three miles: this would have brought him to Streteway Head, giving him a wide view of the rolling countryside to the west. With reason to think that the area was full of rebels Russell surprisingly 'was thoroughly minded and bent to have passed through to the city' but at his moment of decision he was approached by Joll, his household fool, who came running up to him from Honiton. The fool reported that on his way he had heard the bells ringing in the parish church of Honiton, which he presumed was the signal to raise the alarm that the country was up in arms behind him, a situation that Russell had feared from the first day he reached the town. Sending a messenger on to the city with an undertaking that he would be there within a day or two, he returned to his base. After the surprise sprung on him by Smyth's Cornishmen he feared another contingent might debauch on to his troops from the north side of the high road to Exeter.

In the city the situation was critical. The besieged could not understand how Russell's 'coming was not so speedy as was looked for'.[2] No provisioning had been made for the siege that had now lasted nearly a month. It had been a wet July and there had been plenty of water in the springs; dried fish and dried fruit could be had but no bread. 'In this extremity,' Hooker wrote, 'the bakers and householders were driven to seek up their old store of puffins and bran wherewith in times past they were wont to make horse bread and feed their swine and poultry; and this they moulded up in cloths, for otherwise it would not hold together, and so they did bake it up and the people were well contented with it.'[3] Hooker then airs his classical education, quoting Plutarch: *'fames reddit omnia dulcia, nihilque contemnit esuriens.* Hunger makes all things sweet, and the hungry belly shunneth nothing'.

In these straits the common citizens would have been ready to surrender the city, for the majority of them still favoured the rebel cause. Aware of this danger the magistrates imposed a levy for the relief of the poor who were the worst hit by the shortage of supplies: whatever victuals were to be had in the city were to be given to them, either freely or at a very small price. The poor also were the first to receive a share of the spoils whenever stray cattle came close to the city walls and a sortie was made to round them up; even the prisoners were not forgotten and were apportioned their meat, though it was usually horse flesh.

But nerves remained tense. The citizens were weary of the siege. On the last Sunday before the relief of the city an armed company in sympathy with the rebels gathered in the streets about eight in the morning, hoping to raise a tumult against the Protestant party, crying, 'Out, these heretics and these two-penny book men (the price no doubt of the new Prayer Book) ... by God's wounds and blood we will not be pinned in to serve their turn: we will go out and have in our neighbours; they be honest, good and godly men'.(4) As most Protestants were either at home or in church at the time the rioters were easily dispersed before a fight was joined. There was only a small stir at the South Gate, then the leaders were confined to their homes.

The relief of Exeter had now become a matter of extreme urgency. After five weeks of siege the Mayor felt that he had done all he could to defend the city and could hold out not a day longer. He was about to cut his way out when, on Saturday 3 August,

Russell, joined now by Grey's Lanzknechts, artillery and trained men, perhaps rather less than a thousand in all, began his march. Choosing his ground for battle with the eye of an experienced commander he avoided the deep lanes on either side of the direct road to Exeter and turning to the south west over the ground he had covered in his reconnaissance after the battle of Fenny Bridges, he made for the open country towards Woodbury, where his cavalry would have the advantage. On the evening of the same day he was on the heath above Clyst St Mary. He was now only two miles from Topsham at the confluence of the Exe and Clyst, where ships with merchandise for Exeter rode at anchor. From there lay an easy and open road to the city. That night Russell pitched his camp at a windmill belonging to a gentleman, Gregory Carey, which was a prominent landmark on the bleak waste.

But there was a rebel force in the neighbourhood. As soon as it became known that Russell was on the down they attacked. 'Notwithstanding they were of very stout stomachs and very valiantly did stand to their tackles, they in the end were overthrown and the most part of them slain'.[5] Myles Coverdale, Russell's chaplain, then held a service of thanksgiving for the victory: a former Augustinian canon, he had made his name as a preacher against the sacrament of Penance and against the erection of statues in churches. Exiled to the Continent in 1535 he had made the first complete translation of the Bible into English. A most noted orator, he preached a forceful sermon that evening with the rebel dead lying unburied around him in the field. It is likely that he prefaced his sermon with 'The Prayer for men to say on entering battle' which was printed in the Book of Psalms published the year before. Addressing the 'Almighty King and Lord of Hosts', he would have asked God, not too appropriately, to instil in his men 'the courage of the young, unarmed, inexpert David' in confronting 'the great huge Goliath'.

Before Coverdale finished the service an alarm was raised and there was a call for 'every man to his horse and harness again'. The rebels in Clyst, on hearing what had happened at the windmill and fearing they would be attacked next, sent out a call for help. Vast numbers responded from every quarter, several thousand in all.

The next morning, Sunday, Russell decided to attack. Dividing up his army he planned a three-pronged attack on Clyst. The village had been strongly fortified with an outer defence of ramparts behind which the main body of rebels was drawn up on the green. The assault was led by Sir William Francis of Combe Florey in Somerset, followed closely by Russell. Charging at a gallop Francis took the ramparts at the first rush: the defenders broke their ranks and Sir William Francis entered the village. But the houses and walls on either side of the street were lined with archers who worked havoc at close quarters on Sir Williams's men. Worse was in store for them. At the back of the village was a furze brake, where Sir Thomas Pomeroy had taken up his position unobserved. Emerging suddenly, he fell on the German Lanzknechts and the Italian arquebusiers with the English troops fighting with them. Believing themselves surrounded the attacking troops fell back in confusion and were driven up the hill to their camp by the windmill. Russell's cannon, shot and gunpowder were captured and carried back into Clyst. Lacking cavalry, Arundell could not continue the pursuit and complete the rout. Forced to withdraw with the loot he gave time to Russell to re-form his troops. This was perhaps the turning point of the campaign.

For the moment at least the victory of the rebels appeared complete. But Russell rallied his men and advanced towards the village. The rebels again had lined the high banks on either side of the lane sloping down to Clyst. Sir William Francis, once again leading the charge, was clubbed on the head and killed. But from another direction the arquebusiers forced their way into the village, where every house was full of armed men. Unable to give battle, Russell ordered the mercenaries to set fire to every house or building in the street. Driven out into the open the defenders ran into the fire of the arquebusiers. As many as could rallied in the centre of the village where Russell's cavalry tried to charge them down: 'the fight was very fierce and cruel and bloody was that day, for some were slain with the sword, some burned in the houses, some shifting for themselves were taken prisoners,' and many thinking to escape over the river that runs from Topsham to Exeter, which at the time was filled with tidal water, were drowned. Others were cut down on the waterside. Some thousand rebels lost their lives and a large number were taken prisoner.[6]

But in spite of their losses the majority of the rebels made their escape over the bridges, which they had fortified with cannon and felled trees. Determined to make a stand there they alligned their men on the opposite bank. Reluctant to charge the bridges or to

89

attempt to cross the muddy water Grey halted. But luck was with him again. Among his men was a gentleman from the district, John Yarde, who knew of a ford higher up the river by the mill at Bishop's Clyst. Here his cavalry could cross. 'But this was not for all the rest of the army,' explains Hooker, 'who must needs pass over the bridge which then they could not do by reason that the same was so overlaid with great trees and timber. Whereupon a proclamation was made that whosoever would adventure and make way over the bridge would have four hundred crowns for his labour. Then one forthwith more respecting the gain than forecasting the peril gave the adventure, but the gunner rewarded him, for he discharged his piece upon him and slew him'.[7] But, unobserved, another of Grey's men waded across under the bridge and while the gunner was reloading his piece struck him from behind. A party then rushed across the bridge and joined up with the cavalry higher up on the heath. What remained of the rebel army fell back towards Exeter.

Grey, however, happening to look back in the direction of Woodbury Hill, saw what he believed was the glint of armour and thinking mistakenly that a large company of rebels was gathering in his rear, warned Russell. To prepare for what he believed might be an attack he decided to disembarrass himself of the prisoners taken at Clyst and gave orders that they should all be slaughtered. Within the space of ten minutes every one of them was cut down. John Hayward, the chronicler of the reign of Edward VI, puts the number of the slain at nine hundred. That night Russell's army encamped in the open again on Clyst heath to avoid being taken by a surprise attack.

This was warfare as it had been conducted in Germany during the peasant's revolt and explains the loathing in which foreign mercenaries were held in England. Hooker like Hayward simply gives the reason for Russell's order for each man to 'make despatch of his prisoners' his fear if he were 'newly set upon' that night they might turn on their captors.

10. THE RELIEF OF EXETER

When news of the massacre reached the rebel forces encamped round Exeter a large contingent immediately drew away from the city walls and making towards Russell's army entrenched themselves on the lower slopes of Clyst heath. There, close to the highway, working quickly and unseen under cover of darkness through the night, they planted their ordnance.

At dawn the next day, 5 August, they 'discharged their ordnance and shot off their pieces' into Russell's troops encamped on the high ground above. Russell attacked at once. Forming his army into three divisions he sent his pioneers to cut a way through the hedges and enclosed ground and came upon the rebels from the rear. Entrapped on all sides the rebels fought fiercely. 'Valiantly and stoutly they stood to their tackle,' writes Hooker, 'and would not give over as long as life and limb lasted, and yet in the end were all overthrown and few or none left alive. Great was the slaughter and cruel was the fight and such was the valour and stoutness of their men that the Lord Grey reported himself that never in all the wars he had been did know the like nor had fought in so murderous a fray.'[1] There could hardly have been a greater tribute to the valour of the men from Devon and Cornwall, for Grey had led the charge against the Scottish infantry at the battle of Musselburgh in 1547.

After the battle Russell's men marched down the river to Topsham, about a mile away, carrying with them the body of Sir William Francis, which a few days later was borne into Exeter cathedral for burial with full military honours.

The night of the fateful 5 August the rebels remaining round Exeter broke camp and marched away, keeping their order and taking their guns with them, as Russell was to discover later, though to Hooker from inside the city walls they appeared to panic 'as men despairing to prevail', and secretly giving over the siege 'ran apace every man his way'.[2] Without seeking revenge for the massacre of their men by Grey's mercenaries the rebels released the gentlemen whom before the siege they had kept prisoners in churches and other places around the city. Walter Raleigh, who had been held in the tower of St Sidwell's church, went off after looting the building, taking with him a silver cross, a chalice, a thurible and boat, a silver spoon, several rich vestments and the best cope valued at twenty marks. Although the parish tried to recover its treasures, Raleigh would seem to have held on to them. When asked to return the cope he replied that 'if it were not cut already for the sparmer of a bed, they should have it'.[3]

In three days of fighting the rebels had suffered very heavy losses just as the city was on the point of surrendering: five weeks of shortages and suffering had brought the citizens close to starvation. As soon as the gentlemen released from confinement came rushing into the city with the news that the rebels had broken camp, many of the famished citizens rushed out of the gates 'in search of food more than for spoils though they were glad of both, howbeit some did not long enjoy the same, for man being more greedy of meat than measurable in feeding did so overcharge themselves in surfeiting that they did die thereof'.[4]

Very early the next morning, 6 August, Russell ordered his trumpeters to sound the reveille and the troops to prepare for the march. About eight o'clock his army stood before the city walls. However, he did not pass through the South Gate. The Mayor had informed him that there was no food in the city and that he had forbidden any man to enter. Accordingly, Russell pitched his tent outside the walls in St John's Fields next to Southernhay and set up the red dragon of the royal standard on the walls by the postern of his Exeter residence. There the Mayor and the civic dignitaries met him. Russell promised them rewards for their fidelity and wasted little time in keeping his word.

In the course of the same day Sir William Herbert arrived with a thousand Welshmen, 'too late for the fray yet soon enough to the prey', for the whole countryside was then ravaged, a 'just plague of the Lord', in Hooker's judgement, upon the rebels and disloyal persons. Whatever the Welshmen seized in scouring the neighbourhood, they sold cheaply to the citizens, who within two days had sufficient corn, cattle and other supplies for their needs.

The day after Russell camped outside the South Gate there was a faint stirring of a fresh rebellion in his rear. This was something that he had feared might happen during his anxious days of waiting for reinforcements in Honiton. Several men had met in the Crown in Winchester, where they planned a rising for the restoration of the Mass. The leaders were a Winchester carpenter, John Garnham, and a Sussex man called Flynt. At their headquarters in the Crown Inn they worked out the details of their elaborate campaign. The cathedral clergy under duress would provide the funds, three pieces of ordnance were to be seized from Selsey church where they were stored and a thousand men, Garnham reckoned, would answer the call to arms. An order was given for a banner to be made, similar to that of the Western rebels, depicting the Five Wounds, with the chalice and Host and a priest kneeling in adoration. Marching to Salisbury they would behead the Mayor, an arranged signal for Russell's unwilling conscripts to desert, then after joining forces with Arundell, they would turn on Herbert's Welshmen and continue to London. The plot, however, collapsed when Garnham failed to turn up at the appointed meeting place: either he had been arrested or the plot was abandoned on news that Exeter had been relieved.[5]

Russell meanwhile had assumed dictatorial powers, which brought him into conflict with the Council. Taking advantage of the proclamations on forfeitures sent him by the Council in mid-July, he proceeded to award his followers with the estates of the leading rebels even before they were killed or captured. In addition to a large number of smaller grants to numerous followers, he gave Sir Peter Carew all John Wynslade's estates in the two counties; Sir Gawen received Humphry Arundell's lands and Sir William Gibbs John Bury's properties in Hartland, Ugborough, Tavistock and elsewhere; and to some who had served him well he gave 'prisoners, both bodies, goods and lands'.

There is little doubt that Russell treated the captured rebels with far greater severity than the Council demanded. In several places in and around Exeter he set up gallows for all, including priests, whom he regarded as their leaders. Among those who suffered immediate execution was Robert Welsh, the vicar of St Thomas's near the Exe bridge, who had been presented to the benefice by Lord Russell himself, its patron. In spite of the fact that early in the siege he had prevented the Breton gunner from setting fire to the city he was shown no mercy. Among the charges against him was that 'he did not only persuade the people to the contemning of the reformed religion' but that he had kept and observed the Romish religion in his parish. Since Welsh was a highly regarded priest everything was done, presumably by Russell's chaplains, 'to recover him to their opinions, sometimes with fair words, sometimes with threatenings, and sometimes with imprisonments, but he still inveighed against them, calling them both rebels and traitors both against God and the King'.

Welsh's execution was entrusted to Duffield, the leader of the Protestant party on the city Council both before and after the siege. 'Being nothing slack in his commission he caused a pair of gallows to be made and set up upon the top (of the tower) of the said vicar's parish church of St Thomas; and all things being made ready and the stage perfected for the tragedy, the vicar was brought to the place and by a rope about his middle was drawn up to the top of the tower, and there in chains hanged in his popish apparel, and had a holy water bucket and sprinkler, a sacring bell, a pair of beads and such other popish trash about him; and he remained there hanging in this way for a long time, but very patiently he took his death' and did not confess that he had been wrong in fighting for what he believed. 'He had been a good member of his commonwealth' writes Hooker, 'had not the weeds overgrown the good corn'; and he goes on to say that Russell had been severe against such priests whom he rightly regarded as ringleaders, adding that 'to all who did humble themselves he was pitiful and merciful'.[6]

Led to believe from the triumphant tone of Russell's despatch that all was now over, the Council arranged for the relief of Exeter to be celebrated on 8 August with a service of thanksgiving in St Paul's cathedral, at which Cranmer preached. Somerset then proceeded to send out orders and advice to Russell as he had done before the fighting began. Russell was now instructed to turn his attention to the defences on the south coast against the French who had just declared war: he was to guard the ports and all possible landing places in Devon, Cornwall and Dorset and in all places under his jurisdiction, with particular regard to Poole; all ships were to be given licence to put out to sea and destroy French 'merchandise, ship, goods and persons'. Two days later, on 10 August, Somerset, again worried about the empty treasury, judged that it was now safe to disband the army in the West, starting with the men from Somerset and Dorset who would have no zest for a fight against their Devonshire neighbours. And, again, another two days after this he despatched more detailed instructions; Russell was to disband his men in the following order: first the mercenaries: they were to be sent to London and employed abroad, then the horsemen, who were paid twice the daily wage of footmen, and, thirdly, men from distant counties because they were a heavier charge on the Exchequer. To ease further his financial burden Somerset proposed that Russell should prey on the country, unaware that the district had been despoiled already and that the interruption of the harvest by the rebellion had caused a universal shortage of provisions. Finally, clutching at straws, he called Russell's attention to a pirate called Thompson, buccaneering in the River Severn: if he were caught Russell could pardon him at his discretion for a large ransom. Thompson, however, was captured and brought to London on 26 August, a week after the suggestion was made. In the same letter Somerset congratulated Russell on executing the ringleaders, asking at the same time to be given their names.[7]

Somerset was particularly anxious that Humphry Arundell, Wynslade and Underhill should be captured and brought to London so that he could make an example of them that would strike terror into the people and ensure that no further insurrections against the newly established Service Book should occur. At the same time Sir Thomas Pomeroy, who had led the charge at the windmill, should if possible be pardoned, but secretly: this was for reasons personal to Somerset, to whom he had sold his ancestral estates, with the manor, park and castle of Pomeroy. The Protector suggested that when Pomeroy was taken he might be able to do special service in apprehending his fellow rebels, though he would be required first to renounce his popish errors. As a final instruction Russell was told to make enquiries everywhere for papists and to search out the Mass books of the old 'superstitious' services and to see to their destruction.

While Russell was occupied in Exeter the rebels, 'fully bent to maintain their quarrel and to abide the battle', were quietly busy reorganising what remained of their forces about twelve miles away to the north west around Sampford Courtenay, the seedbed of the rebellion in Devon. There, on high ground about a mile to the east of the village they were 'strongly encamped as well by the seat of the ground as by the entrenching of the same'. The main body made ready there to meet the assault of Russell's army, while Arundell with a picked force lay concealed in the village itself. News that the rebels were still at arms in the area would seem to have taken Russell by surprise: Hooker says that he was convinced that the campaign was over, as both his despatches and his concentration on the affairs of the city would seem to bear out.

Marching out from his camp around Exeter on 15 August Russell made only seven miles that day to Crediton: his army was now swollen by Herbert's Welshmen and the gentlemen who had recently joined him, in all a total, on Hooker's reckoning, of seven or eight thousand. In spite of their heavy losses the rebels were ready for battle, though they were 'nothing nor in order nor in company nor in experience to be compared with the others'. That night Russell, who had left his business in Exeter unfinished, wrote to Blackaller ordering him to raise a special levy on the citizens who had been in sympathy with the rebel cause and had not contributed to the city's defences.

Soon after dawn on the following morning there was a skirmish in the lanes in which the shoemaker, Maunders, who had signed the Articles, was captured. Grey and Herbert were then sent forward with a large division of the army and covered another twelve miles to within three miles of the rebel encampment: they were to storm the rebel position while Russell brought up the rear.

The battle began with a cannonade on the advanced rebel trenches, which was returned with what remained of Arundell's ordnance. This exchange won time for the pioneers to cut a way through the high hedges in preparation for a two-pronged assault, on one side by the mercenary footmen, on the other by the Italian arquebusiers. The violence of this attack forced the rebels to fall back on the village, which had been strongly fortified.

Russell was still a long way behind with his heavy train when Arundell made a sudden assault on the rear of the advanced troops attacking the village and threw them into wild confusion. The rebels, wrote Russell in his despatch, 'wrought such fear in the hearts of our men as we wished our power a great deal more, not without good cause'.[8]

To retrieve the situation Grey was forced to leave Herbert to press home the attack on Sampford Courtenay while he himself turned to face Arundell. In the fray Thomas Underhill, the tailor from the village who was sought after by the Council, was slain: it was he who on Whit Monday had confronted Fr Harper on his way to church and had forced him to put on the traditional vestments and offer Mass as it had always been done and not read from the new Prayer Book: he too had signed the Articles sent up to London.

Towards evening Russell reached the scene and organised a renewed assault on the village which was still in rebel hands. Three columns, under Herbert, Grey and himself were to advance simultaneously. Overwhelmed by sheer number the rebels broke and fled. In the pursuit a large number of prisoners were taken. The number of the slain was variously reckoned: Russell estimated that five or six hundred were killed around the camp and another seven hundred in the pursuit, and still greater 'execution had followed had not night come on so fast'.[9] Although a large number of prisoners were taken, many got away. Russell, fearing to be surprised again, remained on horseback with his men all that night.

Arundell attempted to make another stand a few miles to the south at Okehampton, but the pursuit was too close and he fell back on Launceston. A large number who got away made for Somerset, following the Exe valley. They were led by John Bury and one Coffin, a gentleman. They were pursued closely by Peter Carew and Sir Hugh Paulet, who had been appointed by the Council an adviser to Russell. A column of these fugitives was overtaken at Cranmore castle near Tiverton, where they made a stand: those who were taken prisoner were hanged, drawn and quartered on the spot. The rest, lacking ordnance and ammunition and hopelessly outnumbered, were brought to bay on 29 August at Kings Weston in Somerset.* Exhausted by forced marches they were in no condition to withstand Carew's men. After 'great slaughter and execution' they were overwhelmed, leaving a hundred and four men prisoners. Singly or in pairs they were hanged in Bath, Frome, Mells, Glastonbury, Ilminster, Dunster, Milverton, Wiveliscombe and other Somerset towns.

The executions were supervised by Sir John Thynne, the sheriff of Somerset. From the note of a payment made to the executioner at Frome it is clear that they all suffered the penalty of traitors, being drawn and quartered while still alive after hanging a short time: the entry reads that payment was made to the executioner himself and also for irons and for 'woods for the fire to burn the entrails and for a pan and trivet to seethe the limbs'. There were no executions at Bridgwater, North Curry or Minehead, because pardons were given to the rest.

---

* Kings Weston is to the north west of Bristol. The editors of Hooker's History of Exeter have a note: 'or Kenwardston about eight miles from Langport.' This would appear correct.

11. EXECUTIONS IN THE WEST

According to his own account Arundell, making for Launceston and outriding all others on the road, placed himself in the hands of the sheriff, Sir Richard Grenville, who, with other gentlemen, had been imprisoned in the castle in the first days of the rising. Russell, however, had a different story, namely, that Arundell had tried to persuade the keepers of the castle to murder their prisoners and that the keepers instead set free their inmates, who, with the help of the townspeople, held Arundell and four or five other ringleaders captive.

In his despatch after the battle of Sampford Courtenay Russell wrote that he had sent the Carews ahead to Launceston 'to hold the town in stay' while he was hurrying there himself. He had also given orders to all the port officials to stop any rebels attempting to leave the country.

Russell was still nervous and was prepared for further resistance as he approached Cornwall. On 19 August, three days after the battle, he asked the Council to send him a thousand men to land in the rear of the rebels, but all he was offered was a body of two or three hundred men then on board naval vessels off Alderney: they would be instructed to put into Plymouth and disembark them there. In fact, however, there was no further resistance. From the first engagement at Fenny Bridges Hooker calculated the total rebel losses at four thousand men: executions under martial law that had already begun in Exeter before the last battle were eventually to total perhaps another thousand.

Even before receiving the instructions of the Council sent on 11 August to execute 'the heads and stirrers of rebellion ... in so diverse places as you may to the more terror of the unruly', Russell had been active erecting gallows in Exeter and supervising gruesome executions in public with the object of preventing the people attempting 'such kind of rebellion again'.[1] Now, after the last battle, 'minding to make sure of all things,' writes Hooker, 'the Lord Russell marcheth into Cornwall and following his former course causeth execution to be done upon a great many and especially on the bell-wethers and ringleaders'. But while doing this he was to send up to London Sir Thomas Pomeroy with Humphry Arundell, the Mayor of Bodmin and just two of three of the 'most rankest traitors': they were to be closely guarded and, should they attempt to escape, they were to be killed. Any general pardon was temporarily to be postponed. Again, the Council, asserting its belief that religion had been the cause of the insurrection informed Russell that a supply of Prayer Books had been despatched to him for distribution in Devon and Cornwall.

After seeing to the arrest of John Wynslade at Bodmin and of Arundell and others at Launceston, Russell, who had shown himself capable of uninhibited cruelty, returned to Exeter, leaving Sir Anthony Kingston, the Provost Marshal, to continue the work of hanging the rebel leaders, not excluding the priests among them. As a modern historian has written, Kingston relished the task: 'he left an unsavoury name behind him in Cornwall. We have no account of what happened in those grim, tragic days; darkness draws down, lit only by lurid lights'.[2] The barbarity of Kingston's dealings with the rebels did more than prevent any recurrence of a Catholic insurrection in the west. Visiting the county half a century later, another Carew wrote that Kingston 'hath left his name more memorable than commendable amongst the townsmen',[3] but he adds in justification that he 'did nothing therein as a judge by discretion but as an officer by direction'. Sir John Hayward, the chronicler of the reign of Edward VI, on the other hand, attempts no justification: writing less than a hundred years after the rising, he confesses that Kingston was 'deemed by many not only cruel but uncivil and inhumane in his executions.[4]

Hooker gives the names of six priests who were executed: Robert Welsh, vicar of St. Thomas, William Alsa, once vicar of Gulval, Simon Morton, vicar of Poundstock, Richard Benet, vicar of St Yepe and St Neot, Roger Baret, who signed the Articles, and John Tompson; in addition another three are known to have been executed: Robert Bochym, whose brother John had his estate confiscated, and John Barrow and John Woodcock, both mentioned in Holinshed's *Chronicle*. Several other priests are known to have taken part in the Rising: there is a record of one who escaped the gallows, Gabriel Morton, vicar of Lelant: he was handed over as a captive to Kingston: Kingston then made over the tithes and profits of his living to a friend during Morton's lifetime.

The best remembered of them all is Simon Morton, the vicar of Poundstock, a church attractively located in a small hollow surrounded by trees: if he was the vicar responsible for the now-faded wall painting of Christ blessing the local trades, represented by a hammer, saw, sickle and scissors, he was clearly a man in sympathy with the craftsmen who comprised perhaps the greater part of the rebel forces: he is pilloried in the Protestant ballad which was sung in London at the time: it runs:

> Their hope was for help in the Popish Mass
> They would need have hanged up a reservation
> The vicar of Poundstock with his congregation
> Commanded them to stick to their idolatry
> They had much provision and
> great preparation
> Yet God has given our King the victory.

As all the executions were carried out under martial law there exists no record of any trial. There are other priests who may have been executed, as for example, Robert Boyse, the vicar of St Cleer, who was attainted like the vicar of St Keverne, an old trouble-spot. Other vicarages were filled with new incumbents, presumably in the place of priests who had been involved in the Rising.

There are examples of Kingston's cruel and callous proceedings told by the chronicler Richard Grafton, a contemporary who was by no means sympathetic to the rebels: it is likely that he received his information at first hand from witnesses who reported every detail: two of the executions that he describes occurred in or near Bodmin.

Nicholas Boyer, who in Henry Bray's absence was deputy Mayor of Bodmin, had by his own account joined the rebels under duress, was invited with some others by Kingston to dine with him. They were heartily welcomed. Before sitting down to dinner Kingston took the Mayor aside and asked him to see that a pair of gallows was erected quickly so as to be ready for an execution after dinner. While this was being done Kingston and his guests dined lavishly. When the banquet was over Kingston, holding the Mayor by the hand, asked to be taken to the gallows. 'Think you they be strong enough?' enquired Kingston. 'Yes, Sir, they are,' replied the Mayor. 'Well then,' ordered Kingston, 'get you up to them for they are provided for you.' The Mayor cried, 'I trust you mean no such thing to me?' 'Sir,' saith he, there is no remedy. You have been a busy rebel and therefore this is appointed for your reward.' So without any further delay the Mayor was hanged.[5]

It would seem that Kingston wanted to display the cruelty of which he was capable at the traditional assembly place of Cornishmen at times of unrest, for it was at Bodmin also that he committed an injustice for a long time lodged in folk memory. There was a miller in the district who had been very active in the rebellion. When warned of Kingston's coming he called his servant, who was not involved in the rebellion, and told him that he had to leave town. 'If there come any to ask for me,' he instructed him, 'say that thou art the owner of the mill and that thou hast kept the same this four years, and in no wise name not me.' When Kingston arrived at the house and asked for the miller, the servant answered that he was the man and had owned the mill for three years. There and then Kingston ordered the servant to be brought to the next tree and hanged. The poor fellow then pleaded that he was only the miller's servant. 'Well then,' answered the Provost Marshal, 'you are a false knave to be in two tales': then gave orders for him to be hung up. When it was pointed out to Kingston that he had hanged only an innocent servant, he replied, 'What then, could he ever have done his Master better service than to hang for him?'

There are other stories also told of Kingston's calculated callousness. At St Ives, for example, after inviting John Payne, the Mayor or Port Reeve, to dinner, he had a gallows set up outside his house during the meal and when it was over hanged him there. Coming in his progress through the county to the attractive hill town of St Columb Major, Kingston ordered William Mayow to be hanged at the sign post of the town tavern. As the man's crime was not a capital offence his wife was advised by friends to plead with the Provost Marshal for his release from prison. But unfortunately, 'to render herself a more amiable petitioner before the Marshal's eyes, this dame spent so much time in attiring herself and putting on her French hood that her husband was put to death before her arrival'.[6]

No doubt other stories told of Sir Anthony Kingston's grisly humour that are not recorded in Grafton's chronicle were passed on to the next generations. Many Cornishmen, like the miller from Bodmin, no doubt escaped crouching in hiding places and protected by their friends, for a safe refuge across the channel to Brittany was cut off by the French war. Countless innocent people also suffered, for the greater part of Cornwall was given over to the ravages of Kingston's troops. For years to come the people of the county dated their calendar from the time of the Rising. 'After the commotions' and 'after the commotion time' were phrases used in daily speech and in the courts of law.

On 12 September Russell, now back in Exeter, received orders from the Council to see to the removal of all church bells in the counties of Devon and Cornwall: it was said that they had been rung by the rebels 'in every parish as an instrument to stir up the multitude'. To prevent this happening again all bells had to be removed, leaving in each church only one bell, the least of the peal, which would 'serve to call the parishioners together to the sermons and the divine service'. This was to be done 'with as much quietness and as little force of the common people as may be'. The sale of the bells would help to defray the cost incurred by the Treasury in suppressing the rebellion.[7]

It would seem, however, that the commissioners, fearing further disturbances, acted with discretion and instead of removing the bells, took away the clappers or the ironwork frames or both: in many cases the clappers were sold to parishioners: in Morebath, for example, three parishioners paid 26s. 8d. for the clappers, while at Barnstaple, a large borough, the people acquired the clappers for £2.13.4d.[8] For the rest of the reign one small bell summoned the people to church.

From the day he first entered Exeter Russell acted with unrestrained arbitrary power. While gathering his forces at Honiton in July he had been instructed to issue a proclamation threatening the rebels with confiscation of their property and loss of their copyholds if they did not surrender, a measure intended to prevent still greater numbers flocking to banner 'and to stay the multitude from coming forward'. Russell, however, did not interpret the proclamation as a temporary measure, as was clearly intended , but began at once to distribute the lands, copyholds, farms and goods of the rebels to all whom he judged to have served him well. This was a flagrant usurpation of a right that belonged exclusively to the Crown. The Council, not yet informed of the savage treatment of the Cornish rebels, was alarmed, fearing that Russell was preparing the ground for another insurrection. His action, he was cautioned, would lead only to 'sedition, trouble, strife and contention' and, as the event proved, 'rest a grudge not only in the heads of the sufferers but in all other men's judgement of the shire'.[9] On hearing of the ravages of Russell's troops in Cornwall the Council again severely reprimanded him that 'being under government pay ... they might have been well restrained from going to the spoil' for there was danger now of the commons becoming 'much more stirred to follow their devilish practices'.[10] Clearly, in London Somerset was unaware of Russell's determination to make sure that the westcountrymen would never rise again in rebellion.

12. REACTION AND REWARDS

After his capture at Launceston on 19 August Arundell had been taken to Exeter gaol to join the other principal rebel leaders imprisoned there. From there Russell had been ordered to send them, heavily guarded, to London so that they could be examined 'to pick out of them further matter': the party sent up numbered ten and along with Arundell included Sir Thomas Pomeroy, John Wynslade with his son William, Thomas Holmes, a yeoman from Blisland, John Wyse, a gentleman from Launceston, John Bury and Coffin, who had been captured in the last stand at Kings Weston, and William Fortescue, the unidentified member of the well-known Devon family.

The prisoners left Exeter by the East Gate under an escort commanded by Lord Grey: the first few miles took them along the road past Fenny Bridges, the scene of the first battle, then on through Honiton, following in reverse Russell's advance on Exeter. On reaching London on 8 September they were all lodged temporarily in the Fleet prison.

There is no evidence that the rebels, as frequently happened, were paraded in the streets as they approached the city centre. The Council was still nervous of a disturbance in the capital. Already plays had been prohibited for fear they might contain matter tending to sedition or to contempt of good order. A counter attraction to the prisoners had been provided by the Council, for on the same day Edmund Bonner, the Bishop of London, who was suspected of favouring the rebels, was to preach at St Paul's Cross, to give witness to the new orthodoxy.

Bonner had resisted to the last in the House of Lords the introduction of the Prayer Book. After Whit Sunday, the day trouble started at Sampford Courtenay, it had been noticed that he never officiated in English: 'in London and elsewhere he was reported to frequent foreign rites and Masses such as were not allowed by order of the realm'.[1] Commanded by the Council to reside permanently in his London house, he was further ordered to preach a sermon to the satisfaction of the Council, demonstrating that all persons rebelling against the Sovereign incurred damnation, a statement contrary to the traditional teaching that in certain circumstances there could be a just rebellion; and the Bishop was to go on to demonstrate that the rebels in Devon and Cornwall 'were ever to be in the burning fire of Hell with Lucifer, the father and first author of disobedience - what Masses or holy water soever they went about to pretend', and lastly he was to proclaim that 'vital religion consisted only in prayer to God, that rites, forms and ceremonies were but the dress or outward costume which the magistrate might change at his pleasure; (and) that if any man, therefore, persisted any longer in using the Latin service, his devotion was made valueless by the disobedience involved in the practice'.[2]

There was a vast crowd at St Paul's Cross on Sunday 8 September to hear Bonner preach. William Latimer, later Queen Elizabeth's Dean of Peterborough, and John Hooper, her Bishop of Worcester and Gloucester, were present in order to give their report on the sermon to the Council: if Bonner complied that morning, his character was ruined, if he refused to comply he was at the mercy of the Government. In the end he was held not to have given satisfaction. Called before the Council he was imprisoned on 1 October in the Marshalsea where he remained until his release by Queen Mary on 6 August 1553.

In preparation for the arrival of the prisoners in London ballads were being sold in the streets with distorted accounts of the collapse of the insurrection in the west. Only fragments have survived, all in common mocking the Mass and the reservation of the Sacrament, while others made fun of the poor vicar of Poundstock or made a martyr of William Hellyons, who was killed on the steps of the church house at Sampford Courtenay. The crude compositions praised the new Communion Service replacing the old Mass. One piece runs like this:

> The supper of the Lord is (now) set forth truly
> To come and receive which they (the rebels) do
> disdain
> They say that it is a thing that came up newly
> Which shall not continue it may be certain
> For we will sure have the Mass up again
> And God of little might hanged up on high
> For which they have fought and many of them
> slain[3]

Within a few weeks of the arrival of the rebel leaders in London Somerset was swept from power: John Dudley, Earl of Warwick and later Duke of Northumberland, acting with his brother, Thomas Wriothesley, Earl of Southampton, and other members of the Council moved to oust the Protector who was staying with the King, his nephew, in custody at

Hampton Court. About 4 October Somerset had begun to suspect that something was afoot and appealed to Russell to stay by him with his army. Two days later he moved the King for greater safety to Windsor and begged Russell 'to show the part of a true gentleman and of a very friend, for which we trust God will reward you and the King's Majesty in time to come'.[4]

Russell, however, awaited developments and then threw his weight in with Warwick and sealed the fate of Somerset. The Protector, virtual ruler of England, was imprisoned in the Tower. Among the charges brought against him was that he had been the cause of dangerous insurrections in the realm, and had 'suffered rebels and traitors to assemble and to lie in camp in armour against the King, the nobles and gentlemen without speedily repressing them'.

This charge referred both to the western rebellion and to the Rising in Norfolk in the second half of August, after the last battles had been fought round Exeter. Led by Robert Kett, the insurrection there had been caused by agrarian want and misery. Marching from Wymondham, Kett had invested Norwich with some sixteen thousand men. The first force sent by Somerset against him had been routed. It was only when Warwick, Somerset's most powerful colleague, had gathered a powerful army that the rioters were defeated with great slaughter on 27 August. Executions followed, Kett was brought to London for trial and nothing now could prevent Somerset's fall.

Warwick and the new rulers were too concerned in securing their position to pay much attention to Arundell and his fellow prisoners. But sometime before 22 October Arundell and the elder Wynslade, Bury and Holmes were transferred to the Tower where they joined the two priests, Richard Crispyn and John Moreman, whose release had been demanded by the rebels. The fate of Coffin, who was brought up with them from Exeter, is unknown: he may have died of his wounds or he may have been released, though there is no record of it. The remaining five, including Sir Thomas Pomeroy and the younger Wynslade, were set free by order of the Privy Council on 1 November. Some, if not all of them, had surrendered voluntarily and for this reason were pardoned after giving bonds for good behaviour.

Although the prisoners in the Tower had all previously been examined by Russell in Exeter, they were now submitted to further investigation before the Council in an attempt to find incriminating evidence, if not against Princess Mary and Somerset, then at least against Cardinal Pole and perhaps some others. The three examiners included Sir Richard Southwell, the father of St Robert Southwell. Since nothing to their purpose was obtained, there was a further examination in the Tower, not without the suspicion of the use of torture. The report gives little more than an account of the way each of the four was put under duress to join the rebels.

Rather more than a month later, on Tuesday 26 November, all four of the ringleaders lodged in the Tower were taken by boat up river for trial in Westminster Hall. Standing at the bar with them were the captured Norfolk rebel leaders, whose demands in the form of twenty-nine Articles included only three that touched on religion: the rest concerned taxes, enclosures, wardships and other secular or agrarian grievances. It would seem that by bracketing Arundell and his companions with Robert Kett and his followers the Council was anxious to play down the religious character of the western rebellion.

Arundell and Wynslade, according to the indictment read at the trial, had on 19 August put up some resistance at Launceston before their capture. In drawing up the case against Arundell the prosecution appears to have been assisted by John Kestell, who had been summoned from Exeter for the purpose: he was Arundell's servant who 'in the midst of the hottest stirs' sent to the government forces 'so much as he knew of Arundell's proceedings'.(5)

The four prisoners were sentenced to be hanged, drawn and quartered at Tyburn. There was a delay of two months before the sentence was carried out, possibly in the hope of shaking their adherence to the old religion. Kett and his brother, on the other hand, were taken back to Norfolk and hanged at Norwich and Wymondham on 7 September.

Eventually on 27 January 1550 Humphry Arundell, John Wynslade, John Bury and Thomas Holmes were dragged from the Tower on a hurdle for execution at Tyburn. In the crowd that watched them on their way were friends and servants like Rowland Jeynens, a youth of nineteen, and Richard Popham, who had been in Wynslade's service for ten years.

In addition to the party of rebels sent up with Arundell from Exeter, there were others who followed later after a preliminary examination by Russell: some like Humphrey Bonville, who had married John Wynslade's sister, and Thomas a Leigh of St Mary Week, another of Arundell's servants, were released on heavy recognizances. But the fate of others sent up with them is not known. One chronicler states that John Thompson and Roger Baret, who had signed the Articles, and six or seven more priests were hanged at Tyburn.[6]

Sometime after the condemnation of the leaders in Westminster Hall, Cranmer published in the form of a pamphlet his answer to the fifteen Articles of the rebels. Written at the request of the Council when it could no longer be denied in London that the rebels had died for the old beliefs and practices, the language is vitriolic. Addressed in form 'to the ignorant men of Devon and Cornwall', but intended for the rebel sympathisers in the city, Cranmer enquires mockingly what General Council or particular decrees the rebels want to maintain. Then he draws a picture of a priest mumbling in Latin words that no one understands, while some of the congregation listened and the rest walked restlessly up and down the aisles. 'Neither the priest nor the parishioners wot what they say', he writes, and then goes on to give some examples of old devout practices like the blessing of the throat on the feast of St Blaise as a protection against infections of the throat in winter. After all, he claims, he is the person who ought to know about these superstitions for he is the Archbishop of Canterbury.

As a piece of vituperative writing it is Cranmer at his best.

In the same year that the rebel leaders were executed at Tyburn the Act against superstitious books and images was passed by Parliament: all popish books were to be 'utterly abolished, extinguished and forbidden for ever to be used or kept in this realm or elsewhere within any of the

King's dominions'; and any person or body found to possess such books or writings 'or any images of stone, timber, alabaster or earth, graven, carved or painted' taken from any church or chapel and not defaced or destroyed before the last day of June was to be convicted. More than a century later John Aubrey, the antiquary, was told by his grandfather that leaves of illuminated manuscripts from Malmesbury Abbey were used by brewers as stoppers for their casks, by glovers and cobblers for their products, by schoolboys to cover their books and by soldiers to clean their guns.[7] Meanwhile, the chief beneficiaries of the rebellion, the three army commanders, all received vast grants of land and honours. Sir William Herbert, who again had proved himself that 'mad, young, fighting fellow', was raised to the peerage on 10 October 1551 as Baron Herbert of Cardiff, and on the next day was made Earl of Pembroke (second creation). When Somerset fell he acquired Somerset's Wiltshire estates and on the attainder of Sir Thomas Arundell, Humphry's cousin, he was granted Wardour castle and its park, which later reverted to the Arundells.

Lord Russell was rewarded more than abundantly. Firstly, with the fall of Somerset he obtained the Protector's properties in London, which included Long Acre that embraced the site of Covent Garden. On 19 January 1550, eight days before the execution of Humphry Arundell and his companions at Tyburn, he was created Earl of Bedford 'for his assistance in carrying out the order of the Council against images' and for promoting the new religion. Before the end of Edward VI's reign he was granted the Cistercian abbey of Woburn in Bedfordshire, the

Benedictine abbey of Thorney in Cambridgeshire and the Dominican priory (Bedford House) in Exeter. Two and a half centuries later Edmund Burke, the eighteenth century statesman, at odds on one occasion with Russell's descendant, declared that the immense family fortune rested on a series of 'grants so enormous as not only to outrage the economy but even to stagger credibility'.[8]

The city of Exeter was not forgotten. The Mayor, John Blackaller, was given a knighthood, while the city itself was granted the manor of Exe Island: this settled a long-standing dispute with the Earls of Devon, for the people living in the manor had their own laws and their own guards and scorned the authority of the corporation. The grant was regarded as 'a lasting monument to the courage and loyalty of John Blackaller and his brethren'. As an enduring reminder of the deliverance of the city on 6 August, that day, the feast of the Name of Jesus in the Prayer Book, was decreed a day of thanksgiving. Every year for three centuries or more the Mayor, the aldermen and the heads of the corporate trades, wearing their official robes, walked in procession to the cathedral, where the bells were rung and a commemorative sermon preached by one of the Mayor's chaplains. Then, in the reign of Elizabeth I, the city was awarded the motto, *Semper Fidelis*, For Ever Faithful.

With Arundell and his fellow leaders out of the way the reshuffled Council busied themselves in introducing further radical changes in religion. Within a few weeks of the executions at Tyburn, a new Ordinal was produced and the bishops who stood out against it, notably Tunstall of Durham, Heath of York and Gardiner of Winchester, were deprived of their sees and Protestants put in their place.

In April 1550 Nicholas Ridley, the Bishop of Gloucester, was translated to London, where a month after his enthronement he gave orders for all altars in the churches of his diocese to be removed and replaced by 'the Lord's board after the form of an honest table decently covered in such a place of the choir or chancel as shall be thought most meet'. In June the order was given for the setting up of similar tables in all the churches throughout the country and the Lords Lieutenant were commissioned to see that this was done. In Exeter Bishop Vesey was commanded to prepare the people for the transformation of their churches by sermons, both in the cathedral and in all populated areas, but it was not until the old conservative Bishop was replaced by Myles Coverdale, the chaplain to Russell's forces, that the order was enforced. In troubled Cornwall the order was so promptly and efficiently enforced that there is hardly a stone altar to be seen today in any church in the entire county; and with the removal of the altar all lights were extinguished before the rood screens. After the suppression of the Rising all resistance to change in religion was effectively quashed: only Princess Mary dared to resist the government to the end.

The way was now cleared for the introduction of the Second Prayer Book. It is uncertain to what extent Cranmer was responsible for this ultimate measure of disassociation from the old faith. The changes on the Eucharist were significant, coming as they did still closer to the teaching of Zwingli, whose influence was discernible in the First Prayer Book. The word Mass was omitted. Catholic vestments were replaced by the surplice; the words used in the administration of Holy Communion in their primary sense implied that it was no more than a service of remembrance: 'Take and eat this in remembrance that Christ died for thee and feed on him in thy heart by faith and thanksgiving'. Everything that was no longer needed for the simplified worship - chalices, crucifixes of gold and silver, pyxes, candlesticks, thuribles or censers, embroidered chasubles and copes - was confiscated to the Crown.

As with the First Prayer Book its successor was enforced by an even more punitive Act of Uniformity, with a steeper grade of fines for non-attendance at church, culminating in imprisonment. Nevertheless, the preamble to the Act indicates that resistance was still active, referring as it does to 'people in divers parts of the realm (who) do wilfully and damnably ... abstain and refuse to come to their parish churches'. In fact this Second Prayer Book, with some important changes made by Elizabeth I in 1559, remained substantially the Prayer Book of the Church of England.

In the West Russell was one of the six commissioners appointed in January 1551 to make a survey of the church plate, jewels, ornaments and money in Cornwall: he was to forward everything to the Jewel House, leaving only one chalice in each church and perhaps two in the larger churches. After leaving sufficient linen for the altar table he could distribute the rest among the poor.

13. ELIZABETHAN AFTERMATH

The resolute attachment of the commons of Cornwall and Devon to the old faith survived the brutal suppression of the rebellion well into the second half of Elizabeth's reign. Among the indications of this is the report of the visitation of Exeter College, Oxford in 1579: it was then noted with alarm that of the eighty students then in the college 'there were found but four obedient subjects; all the rest (being) secret or Roman affectionaries ... These were such as chiefly came out of the western parts where Popery prevailed'.[1] But within three more generations the two counties that had rebelled against the imposition of the Prayer Book had become solidly Puritan.

Among those who played a leading part in this break with the past was Francis, second Earl of Bedford, who succeeded his father in 1555. He had witnessed the deed of Edward VI by which the crown was settled on Lady Jane Grey. On the accession of Mary he had been imprisoned, but escaped and fled to Geneva. On returning to England on her death he became one of the architects of the Elizabethan religious settlement. He was also a close friend of Peter Martyr, whose teaching on the Eucharist at Oxford had caused riots in the neighbouring countryside. Standing high in the Queen's favour, it was reported by the Spanish ambassador at her court that he and William Cecil were the two members of the Privy Council who busied themselves most earnestly in destroying the old faith.[2] Appointed Lord Lieutenant of Devon, Dorset and Cornwall, Francis Russell threw his paramount influence in these counties behind the Protestant Reformation.

In this endeavour Russell was well supported by John Jewel. A Devonshire man from Buden he had been educated under different teachers at Bampton, South Molton and Barnstaple. Going up to Merton College at the age of thirteen he later became a Fellow of Corpus. On the accession of Mary he had refused to attend Mass, went into exile, staying, together with Russell, as the guest of Peter Martyr at Strasbourg. On his return to England in 1559 he was appointed commissioner for the visitation of the Exeter diocese and in the same year made Bishop of Salisbury. In the course of his visitation he purged the cathedral chapter of its strong Catholic sympathisers, removing the Dean, Sub-Dean and Treasurer, and finally the Bishop himself, James Turbeville, who, on refusing the oath of Supremacy, was sent to the Tower and after a period on bail was thought to have died there. All important positions in the diocese were then filled with radical reformers, like Richard Tremayne from the Protestant Devonshire branch of the family, who had been the proctor of the Exeter clergy in the convocation of 1562: Tremayne abolished all saints' days and 'all curious singing and the playing of organs and the use of the cross at baptism.[3]

Writing in April or May that year to tell Martyr of his commission, Jewel rejoiced that 'the nobility with united hearts and hands are restoring religion throughout the country in spite of all opposition'.[4] What he meant by the restoration of religion is clear from another letter to Peter Martyr written in August the same year reporting recent events in Scotland: 'all the monasteries are everywhere levelled to the ground', he tells his friend excitedly, 'the theatrical dresses, the sacrilegious chalices, the idols, the altars are consigned to the flames; not a vestige of the ancient superstition and idolatry is left.'[5]

Travelling 'now with one foot on the ground, the other almost on my horse's back', Jewel's visitation took him to Gloucester, Bristol, Bath, Wells, Exeter and into Cornwall. In the South West he encountered a very different situation. In Devonshire, for instance, he found no alacrity for reform or for the removal of what he regarded as 'the scenic apparatus of divine worship'. Mass priests, as he calls them, were absenting themselves from the new services as though they were 'the greatest impiety'; and he could only write sadly to Peter Martyr that 'those very things that you and I have laughed at are now seriously and solemnly entertained ... as if Christian religion could not exist without them'.[6]

In his letter in search of sympathy from Peter Martyr, Jewel laments 'the wilderness of superstition that has sprung up in the darkness of Marian times', and mentions as an example the nails which pierced Christ's side on the cross, a clear reference to the emblems of the passions which were emblazoned on the banner of the western rebels. Inadvertently he pays tribute to the loyalty of priests to the old faith, complaining of their 'inveterate obstinacy everywhere'.[7]

When the visitation was over Jewel warmly accepted the offer of help from Russell in 'establishing pure religion' in Devonshire, where Russell had such a large stake in it. 'The Lord Russell lately asked me,' he wrote in yet another letter to Martyr, 'in what way he could most oblige both yourself and others, your brethren and fellow ministers ... I told him that nothing could be more acceptable ... than for him studiously and boldly to promote the religion of Christ and repress the insolence of the papists. This he promised to do and certainly does as far as lies in his power'.[8] To Henry Bullinger, the Swiss Reformer, who had succeeded Zwingli as Pastor of Zurich and was regarded as something of an oracle by the early Elizabethan bishops, Jewel wrote joyously that 'Cecil favours our cause most ardently', a bonus 'for true religion', which compensated for the lack of support in the universities.[9] 'At Oxford,' he wrote in another place, 'there are scarcely two individuals who think with us, and even they are so dejected and broken in spirit that they can do nothing'.[10]

It is difficult to exaggerate the influence of aristocratic patrons in the establishment of 'true religion'. The Carews, Dennises, Grenvilles, Pollards, Raleighs and others who had been active in their support for Russell played a crucial role in imposing the reformation upon the South West. Officially and unofficially they were busy suppressing the old faith of the people. Once again, as had happened in King Edward's reign, they could be found demolishing crosses, seizing church plate, overturning altars and defacing the few images that remained; officially they could regulate both ecclesiastical and secular appointments and even intervene directly in small towns in the appointment of schoolmasters who could be relied on to enforce the injunction of Elizabeth I that no other religion was to be taught except that 'now truly set forth by authority'. Puritans to a man, Russell, Huntingdon and Robert Dudley, Earl of Leicester, the Queen's favourite, exercised to the full their almost unlimited power of patronage in the instalment of Puritan preachers to replace clergy suspected of attachment to the old faith. Russell himself worked in close alliance with Leicester, who could boast that 'there is no man I know in this realm that has shown a better mind to the furthering of true religion that I have done from the first day of her Majesty's reign to this'.[11] In the South West this overwhelming pressure which was brought to bear on the old faith lasted throughout the reign.

In praising the 'nobility' of the South West for their support in his visitation, Jewel touched on another principal cause of the falling away of the commons of Devon and Cornwall from their traditional faith in the years following the rebellion. In places where the old religion was to survive in strength, as for instance in Lancashire, the southern Midlands, Yorkshire and also, well into the eighteenth century, in East Anglia, this was principally due to the considerable and sometimes powerful landowners who were able to maintain priests in their homes to serve their family, retainers and the neighbouring countryside. In Cornwall, Devon and Somerset the situation was different. There, the large estates, often former monastic properties, were either in the hands of non-residents or belonged almost entirely to the Protestant gentry, to the Grenvilles, Godolphins and Edgcumbes in Cornwall and to the Carews, the Tremaynes, Fortescues and Pollards in Devon. The rebellion had ruined the Arundells of Helland, the Wynslades, the Beckets and others: William Wynslade, who had been pardoned after fighting alongside his father, was reduced to leading a roving life playing on his Cornish harp to entertain his gentlemen friends, who dubbed him Sir Tristram.

Heavy fines for non-attendance at church further impoverished such families who might otherwise have provided a refuge for priests. Over the years only a family like the Arundells of Lanherne was able to endure an annual payment of £260 to the Treasury; others like the Beckets were imprisoned for non-payment and at the same time forfeited two thirds of their land; finally, John Becket, the head of the family, was outlawed for debt at the end of Elizabeth's reign; and there was no relief from the sustained oppression in the next reign.

Attachment to the traditional faith totally ruined the Tregians of Golden Manor in central Cornwall. Francis, the head of the family, a courtier and poet, provided a shelter for Cuthbert Mayne, a native of Barnstaple and the first of the seminary priests. From Tregian's house Mayne, in the guise of his servant, ministered to the country people wherever he could find shelter. But the manor was raided in force by the sheriff, Sir Richard Grenville, the son of the Grenville imprisoned by the rebels during the insurrection. His ire against Catholics roused, he saw to the condemnation of Mayne on the evidence of possessing some articles of devotion and had him hanged, drawn and quartered at Launceston on 30 November 1577; Tregian, who was imprisoned in the castle dungeon there, lost his entire property and could only go into exile in Lisbon, where he died revered as a saint. Grenville saw to it that it became impossible for any but the Arundells of Lanherne to sustain a priest anywhere in the county.

On the other hand there was no lack of Cornishmen who became priests abroad and returned to England at the risk of incurring the penalty for treachery. But virtually not one of them, it seems, found it possible to work in the two counties that rose in rebellion in 1549. This alone says much for the severity of the persecution in Cornwall. While it was the practice for incoming priests to find their way to their native county where their regional accent would arouse no suspicion, the Cornishmen had no choice but to work in an unfamiliar part of the kingdom where their speech frequently betrayed them. In the year of Mayne's execution, for instance, two Cornishmen were ordained at Douai, John Curry and John Tippett. Curry, a poor lad from Bodmin, worked from Chideock, a recusant stronghold in Dorset; Tippett from St Wenn, of yeoman stock, was discovered in London after a year in England; another Tippett became a Carthusian monk.

It was about the time of Mayne's execution that two parish clergy renounced their livings and crossed to the seminary at Douai; Thomas Bluet, Rector of St Michael Penkevil, and John Vivian of St Just: neither made it back to Cornwall. Both were arrested. Bluet was imprisoned at Wisbech and Vivian, who was despatched into exile, became a Bridgetine monk. The enrolment of Cornishmen in the seminaries continued to the end of the reign: between 1582 and 1585 three more youths from Cornwall became priests: David Kemp of St Minver who studied at Rheims, was captured and held in York, his cousin Francis Kemp, who entered at Valladolid, and John Cornelius, a poor lad of Irish parentage in the service of Sir John Arundell: he became a student at Exeter, studied in Rome and worked from Chideock until captured and executed at Dorchester in July 1594. The case of John Hambley from St Mabyn, near Bodmin, is unusual. Arriving from the Continent in 1584 he worked zealously in London, but had the misfortune of being captured on a visit to Chard: arraigned at the assizes in Taunton his nerve gave way and he was reprieved after making a full confession, naming his fellow students at Rheims, Vivian, Curry and Trewethan, all Cornishmen. Uneasy in conscience he was reconciled, again arrested and endured martyrdom at Salisbury in April 1587. Like so many young Cornish priests he was never able to work in the county where he was born.

The flow of students to the Continent continued to the end of the reign and beyond: yet another Kemp, Boniface, a Benedictine monk, died a prisoner in York gaol sometime in 1642. The contribution of Cornwall to the English Catholic resistance was at least as great as that of any other county and all the more remarkable because, in the absence of priests, there was only the memory of the rebellion of 1549 to sustain the old faith: a tragic chapter in the history of the kingdom that surely proves how deeply the old religion was entrenched and how limited was the support for the reform.

The suppression of the rebellion signalled the decline of religious devotion among the people of Devon and Cornwall, which was symbolised in the banner of the Five Wounds behind which they marched on Exeter. After little more than a passage of a single lifetime it was replaced by decent conformism, religious inactivity and widespread disinterest.

BIBLIOGRAPHY

The main source for the rebellion is the account by John Hooker (or Vowell) printed as a supplement to Hooker's edition of *Holinshed's Chronicle* (1587) and in the same author's *Description of the City of Exeter* edited by W.J. Harte in the Devon and Cornwall Record Society (1919) which I have used here. To avoid an excessive number of references it can be taken that the occasional phrase or sentence in the text is taken from Hooker's work. The other important contemporary source are the letters of the Privy Council, mainly to Lord Russell, concerning the rebellion and printed in *Troubles Connected with the Prayer Book of 1549* edited by N. Pocock in the Camden Society (1884). And lastly the State Papers Domestic of Edward VI. The two principal secondary sources are Frances Rose-Troup's *The Western Rebellion of 1549* (1913) and A.L. Rowse's *Tudor Cornwall* (1941).

Other works which I have used include:

Ayre, John, *The Works of John Jewel* (Parker Society, Vol.40, 1850).
Carew, Richard, *Survey of Cornwall* (ed. 1811).
Clark, Francis, *Eucharistic Sacrifice and the Reformation* (1960).
Cornwall, Julian, *Revolt of the Peasantry 1549* (1977)
Dickens, A.G. *The English Reformation* (1964).
Duffy, Eamon, *The Stripping of the Altars: Traditional Religion in England 1400-1580* (Yale 1992).
Finberg, H.R.P., *Tavistock Abbey* (Cambridge 1951).
Froude, J.A., *History of England*, vol. iv (1893).

Gilbert, Davies, *Cornwall* , vol.2 (1820).

Hoskins, W.G. and Finberg, H.R.P., *Devonshire Studies* (1954).

Hughes, Philip, *The Reformation in England* , vol.2 (1953).

Pocock, Nicholas, 'The Condition of Morals and Religious Belief in the Reign of Edward VI' in *The English Historical Review* ,No.39 (1895).

Polwhele, Richard, *History of Devonshire* , vols. 1 & 2, (Exeter, 1793-1806)

Ridley, Jasper, *Thomas Cranmer* (Oxford 1962).

Rowse, A.L. & Henderson, M.I., *Essays in Cornish History* (Oxford 1935).

Scarisbrick, J.J., *The Reformation and the English People* (Oxford 1985).

Sturt, John, *The Revolt in the West: The Western Rebellion of 1549* (Exeter 1987).

Tanner, J.R., *Tudor Constitutional Documents 1485-1603* (Cambridge 1951).

Whiting, Robert, *The Blind Devotion of the People: Popular Religion and the English Reformation* (Cambridge 1989).

Youings, Joyce, 'The South-Western Rebellion of 1549', in *Southern History*, Vol.1 (1979).

REFERENCES

Abbreviations

Hooker : *History of Exeter* (Devon and Cornwall Record Society, 1919).
R-T : Rose-Troup, The Western Rebellion of 1549 (1913).
Pocock : *Troubles connected with the Prayer Book Rebellion of 1549* (1884).
Rowse : A.L. Rowse, *Tudor Cornwall* (1941).
Froude : J.A. Froude, *History of England*, Vol.4 (1893).
S.P. Dom: *State Papers Domestic.*

Chapter 1

1. A.G. Dickens, *The English Reformation* (1964), 207.
2. A.L. Rowse and M.I. Henderson, *Essays in Cornish History* (1935), 79.
3. Froude, 98.
4. R-T, 47-59.
5. Ib. 80.
6. Richard Carew, *Survey of Cornwall* (ed. 1811), 177.
7. Rowse, 259.

Chapter 2

1. S.P. Dom. Ed. VI, no.31.
2. *Relation of the Island of England* in R-T, 116.
3. Eamon Duffy, *The Stripping of the Altars* (1992), 97.
4. A.G. Dickens, *The English Reformation* (1964), 219.

Chapter 3

1. Hooker, 56.
2. R-T, 98.
3. Ib. 108.
4. Ib. 337.
5. Richard Carew, *Survey of Cornwall* (ed. 1811), 64.
6. *Ibid.*

Chapter 4

1. Hooker, 57.
2. Ib.
3. Richard Carew, *Survey of Cornwall* (ed. 1811), 187.
4. Ib.
5. Ib. 188.
6. Hooker, 58.
7. A. Jenkins, *History of Exeter* (1806), 112.
8. R-T, 128.
9. J. Cornwall, *Revolt of the Peasantry* (1977), 96.
10. R-T, 128.
11. Pocock, 1.
12. R-T, 154.
13. Pocock, 5.
14. John Vowell (Hooker), *The Life and Times of Sir Peter Carew* (1857), 115.
15. Pocock, 13.

Chapter 5

1. Hooker, 60.
2. Froude, 411.
3. Hooker, 61.
4. Ib. 63.
5. Ib. 65.
6. Ib.
7. Ib. 68.
8. Pocock,
9. *Ibid.*
10. Note in churchwarden's accounts: R-T, 323n.
11. Froude, 420.

Chapter 6

1. Hooker, 68.
2. Ib.
3. Ib. 71.
4. Ib. 85.
5. Vowell (Hooker), *Life and Times of Sir Peter Carew* (1857), 52.

Chapter 7

1. Froude, 423n.
2. R-T, 322.
3.R-T, 323.
4. Ib.
5. Ib. 326.
6. Pocock, 31.
7. Ib. 33.
8. Ib. 35.
9. Hooker, 83.
10. R-T, 215.
11. Rowse, 287.
12. Pocock, 172.

Chapter 8

1. Hooker, 91.
2. Ib. 93.
3. Ib. 71.
4. Ib. 73.
5. Ib. 79.
6. S.P. Dom. Edward VI, vol. viii, no. 32.
7. Froude, vol. iv, 425.
8. Philip Hughes, *The Reformation in England*, vol.2 (1953), 139.

Chapter 9

1. Hooker, 84.
2. Ib. 85.
3. Ib. 79
4. Ib. 75.

5. Ib. 85.
6. Ib. 87.
7. Ib. 88.

Chapter 10

1. Hooker, 89.
2. Ib.
3. Eamon Duffy, *The Stripping of the Altars*, 488.
4. Hooker, 90.
5. J. Cornwall, *Revolt of the Peasantry (1549)*, 188.
6. Hooker, 94.
7. Pocock, 61.
8. Rowse, 281.
9. Ib.
10. R-T, 318.

Chapter 11

1. Pocock, 54.
2. Rowse, 283.
3. R-T, 310.
4. Hayward, *Edward VI* (Camden Society 1840), 65.
5. Pocock, xxvii.
6. R-T, 310.
7. Pocock, 73.
8. R-T, 376.
9. Pocock, 70-71.
10. Ib.

Chapter 12

1. Froude, 423.
2. Ib. 424.
3. R-T, 338.
4. Pocock, 83.
5. R-T, 342n.
6. R-T, 355n.3.
7. J.F. Betty, *The Suppression of the Monasteries in the West Country* (1989), 120.
8. H.P.R. Finberg, *Tavistock Abbey* (1951).

Chapter 13

1. W.G. Hoskins and H.P.R. Finberg, *Devonshire Studies*, 294.
2. H.N. Birt, *The Elizabethan Settlement*, 294.
3. Ib. 367.
4. J. Jewel, *Works*, vol. 4 (Parker Society), 1210.   The letter is undated.
5. Ib. 1215.
6. Ib.
7. Ib. 1217.
8. Ib. 1213.
9. Ib. 1225.
10. Ib. 1213.
11. Patrick Collinson, *English Puritanism* (Historical Association [1983]), 27.

INDEX